HIDING FROM MYSELF

My Complicated Rebirth into Womanhood and My Own Skin.

AMBER ROSE WASHINGTON

Testimonials

"As the father of a transgender woman, I have never used the word journey so much in my life. We started in one place and wondrously ended up in another, more beautiful, exciting, and happier place.

Reading Amber's book reminded me that everyone takes a different path to get to where they want. The beauty of *Hiding From Myself* is that the insecurities and fears that Amber had to successfully overcome are the very same that stops all of us from reaching our destinations.

Everyone can learn from this book, no matter your gender, sexuality, race, or myriad of other characteristics that make us who we are.

This is a warm, funny, educational, and very human story and during this time in history, a reminder that we are all just humans trying to be our best. And that, like this book, is a precious thing."

Colin Mochrie, Actor/Comedian/Producer
"Whose Line is it Anyway"

"This book will forever change your understanding of what it is to be unapologetically you."
Adam Glass, TV Writer/Executive Producer

"Amber's personal story is one of tremendous strength and determination, in the midst of prejudice and personal deprecation, she has battled with incongruity every day. Amber's honest and insightful book will touch your heart as you encounter the many roadblocks and life-changing events she has experienced. How she has faced the world and never been beaten, continually putting herself on the line and fighting for what is rightfully hers.

With Amber's unique perspective of the male world as a transgender woman and as a loving dad she is a wonderful role model to the transgender community and to our society as a whole. This is a must-read for us all as we continue to learn the art of acceptance and embrace diversity—as we are all in ourselves unique."
Vivienne Mason, Author, "Onion Girl"

"As I read this amazing book, I realized as different as I felt growing up, my story is so similar to Amber's. If you grew up transgender thinking you were alone, this is a must-read! You will find yourself in these pages over and over again!"
Taylor Chandler Walker, Trans Activist & Speaker

"As a transgender woman, this book connects with me profoundly. As a friend of the author, I am inspired by the fearlessness with which Amber shares her personal journey. As a writer, I am envious of her grace and style on the page. But ultimately, as a human being, I am deeply moved by every word in this book. In many ways this feels like a history of my own life, but told from Amber's unique and illuminating perspective. Even if you are not transgender and do not know much about the subject, this memoir will provide you with a rich and rewarding experience filled with life, love, and self-discovery."
Rebecca Swan, Screenwriter/Producer

"*Hiding From Myself* is the stirring portrait of a woman risking everything to find—and free—her truest self. A modern-day renaissance woman, Amber Rose Washington's uplifting treatise on the inestimable value of a life fully realized promises not just a window into the transgender experience, but a singularly unique glimpse into the human condition as well."
Yael Boyle, Author, "Sweet Like Snake Wine"

"Amber's life story is so inspiring! I was so intrigued with her thoughts that I couldn't wait to read what she wrote next. A real page turner. This book is going to help so many people understand what it's like growing up transgender. Thank you Amber for sharing your story with the world."
Christine Rizzo, Author & Certified Mindset Coach

"Wow! This book will help SO MANY!!! Sharing your story to help others is the ultimate in vulnerability. This book is such a wonderful gift to others!"
Priscilla Nelson, Certified Health Coach and Author

"Amber's poignant story of inspiration is rooted in circumstance few among us have experienced firsthand, yet her raw emotion lays bare the very fabric of our own existence. As she invites us to share in her transformative journey, the lessons learned along the way serve as encouragement for each of us to overcome the obstacles on the path towards our best, most authentic selves."

Moriah Ritterman

"This is a life-changing book, in the most literal sense. Amber Rose Washington is a force to look up to. Anyone facing any challenge or crisis in life will learn from her honesty, warmth, brilliance, humor, and commitment to be her very BEST self."

Linda Bottaro

"Reading Amber's book was an amazing, enlightening, and at times a frustrating set of events that led her to her journey of authenticity and congruity. She uses her voice to invite the reader into her world of disappointment, frustration, and hope. If you want to understand the complexities a transgender person faces before and during transition, this must-read book provides a detailed, no-bullshit account of her experiences that will leave you emotionally invested."

Sara Fackelman, Ph.D., LMHC, CAP,
Board Certified Gender Therapist,
Certified Clinical Sexologist

For Mom.

As you now watch over me, know that you showed to me

the abiding love of an incredible mother, even when faced with an unknown. Thank you for later giving me the pep talk and strength I needed to face my lifelong struggle head-on unapologetically. I miss you every day my sweet mom.

– and –

Dad, who like Mom, has shown me the unconditional

love every parent should possess. I am proud that you are my dad and that you have gotten to know your other daughter. You are not only my dad add but also my greatest ally and friend in this crazy world.

First published by Ultimate World Publishing 2020
Copyright © 2020 Amber Rose Washington

ISBN

Paperback - 978-1-922372-82-6
Ebook - 978-1-922372-83-3

Amber Rose Washington has asserted her right under the Copyright, Designs and Patents Act 1988 to be identified as the author of this work. The information in this book is based on the author's experiences and opinions. The publisher specifically disclaims responsibility for any adverse consequences, which may result from use of the information contained herein. Permission to use information has been sought by the author. Any breaches will be rectified in further editions of the book.

All rights reserved. No part of this publication may be reproduced, stored in or introduced into a retrieval system, or transmitted in any form, or by any means (electronic, mechanical, photocopying, recording or otherwise) without the prior written permission of the author. Any person who does any unauthorised act in relation to this publication may be liable to criminal prosecution and civil claims for damages. Enquiries should be made through the publisher.

Cover design: Ultimate World Publishing, Amber Rose Washington
Layout and typesetting: Ultimate World Publishing
Editor: Marinda Wilkinson
Cover photo credit: givaga-Shutterstock.com

Ultimate World Publishing
Diamond Creek,
Victoria Australia 3089
www.writeabook.com.au

Author's Note

It is my hope that in writing this book, several generations of readers will gain a fresh perspective on what it is like to grow up incongruent—to grow up transgender. Although times and circumstances change, incongruity remains the common experience for people born like me. In fact, today's trans youth are already facing a more divisive and insidious foe. A foe now emboldened with newly evangelized prejudice, mythology, and misinformation.

My goal is to be a voice for the plain Jane, non-celebrity status transgender person; a comforting shoulder for the frightened; and an example of what not to do when given the life you never asked for. But most of all, I hope that through the lessons I learned, my story becomes a beacon of light in the darkness. A place where you can learn to overcome extreme adversity, conquer your fears, and live your best life unapologetically; transgender or not.

Understand, this book represents *my* truth, *my* history, and *my* unconventional and painful journey into and through womanhood. I can provide you with a unique perspective along with intimate details into many of my life's events. This is possible thanks to several journals, where since early childhood I have documented decades of events, emotions, and dreams. Where there were events

Hiding From Myself

that only remained in my memory, I sought others from my past to get their perspective or recollection. There are a lot of conversational quotes within this book, and while I recall the general conversations, I expanded most of the direct quotes to show you, the reader, greater detail and context contained within the specific event or events.

Many featured within this book have given me permission to use their names. However, there are several other people featured that have had their names changed to protect their privacy, regardless of their positive or negative impact on my life.

I understand that there is no one-size-fits-all journey or story for being transgender. We are all the same, yet different. So once again, this is *my* truth; *my* journey; *my* life experience. Therefore, my experiences should not be perceived in any way that this is the only way to be *trans*. Being transgender has been a living hell on Earth for me. In my heart, I believe none of us enjoy this experience. We would all have rather been born congruent for sure. Mine is just one persona; one narrative out of countless thousands that could be told. So I am grateful and honored that you have decided to read my story.

So to all of you out there fighting the fight, moving forward each day on your own personal journeys—stay strong, be confident, and above all, be unapologetically you.

With love,
Amber Rose

Introduction

How the hell did I go from being a shy, do no wrong, and deeply loved child to a grown woman dis-invited to Christmas with the relatives? It was just as well since I was already busy running from their plan of giving me a good old-fashioned Catholic exorcism.

Boy, oh boy, you bet your ass that would be a party to crash. There's no question my unconscious born and bred Catholic guilt told me I needed to go to confession. I needed forgiveness for the countless terrible choices, "ahem", sins I had committed again and again and again trying to avoid *myself*. But God-dammit, who I was—well, that was never a choice and definitely not worthy of confession. Let alone an exorcism, dare I say, "For Christ's sake."

Yep. That's a small part of why I am religiously agnostic. I believe in what we call God or Source, or The Collective, and consider myself spiritual—I'm just not down with the man-made, age-old mythologies and countless wild interpretations. While I understand religion in any form is, on the surface, well-intentioned, it also has the propensity to turn people into fucking nutbags.

Barring religion from the conversation for a moment, I suppose one could say I had an interesting life. To most people's standard of interest, mine qualified, in some small way, as the bee's knees. I was in and out of the music business, writing and producing music and enjoying a modicum of success in the meantime. People all over the United States heard my music. And although dysphoric to me, my voice was tragically and ironically deep. You know the voice. It's that deep announcer's voice that comes out even when you're just having a simple conversation. The voice that makes people ask, "Wow, are you that voice I hear on the radio?" or "Have you ever thought about doing voice-overs for concerts?" I had the makings of the movie trailer voice; much like (but never came close to) the late master voice artist, Hal Douglas. My voice, while deep, needed dizzying amounts of vocal training. That training got me started in radio voice-over work and live concert intros, warming up crowds of up to 8,000 people.

I had to fit into that male persona, steer myself away from my true gender identity, and blend in. I needed to compensate, and that was my ticket. That's how many of us do it, you know? We attempt to compensate, but almost always end up overcompensating.

All of this newfound exposure had me meeting, befriending, and working with a lot of famous people. Yep. I was on my way to big things. Yawn.

People often say to me, "Wow! Your life has been so interesting."

In the past, I would agree and continue to talk it up and name-drop even more. God, how pathetic was I? I didn't fit in in any conventional way, so hamming it up about famous people, some of whom I barely knew, seemed to give me the attention I needed. That "interesting life" bullshit was all I had. Especially since I had nothing else going for me that was authentic—not even me.

The catharsis I experienced while reliving my life through this memoir dramatically altered my responses.

Introduction

They became, "If you want me to be honest? All of that interesting life stuff means zilch when you don't have the luxury of being the real you."

I realized those experiences with dozens of famous people were as fake as the persona I wore for decades. Not because those experiences didn't happen, but because I wasn't living an authentic life. I know this because I finally gave Amber her freedom.

People often jump to the wrong conclusion with people like me. They often say, "Good for you . . . as long as you're happy." Life isn't binary, nor is it two-dimensional. We are neither happy nor sad. Rather, we are many things on a multitude of levels. So the phrase, "as long as you're happy," has nothing to do with my transition. It's about overcoming the extreme fear within you that knows a fair percentage of society is hell-bent on being shitty to you. It's about learning and growing, both spiritually and emotionally. It's about allowing the person inside you the freedom to take their first real breath. And at its very core, at least for me, it's about—affirmation.

Prior to my successful transition, my life was a huge, disastrous, hot mess, chock-full of massive insecurity, heartache, and longing. I experienced dread, regret, anger, and sadness with each rite of passage I had missed growing up. My insecurity allowed me to be the victim of emotional, mental, and physical abuse. I was profoundly good at making poor choices. Choices that guaranteed countless failed relationships and three divorces that affected four beautiful children. Then there was a myriad of health issues most people will never have to experience in their lifetime, causing anxiety on a level I didn't know existed. Yeah, I had happiness glitter sprinkled all over me.

Okay. I can't be a complete drama queen and portray my life as some pathetic (roll your eyes now) "boo-hoo" session. There were times, as unnatural as they felt, that, "I had me one hell of a ride" in what I call boy mode.

The most troubling and destructive part of my life had to do with the relentlessness of trying to replace *him*. I never realized the profound effect he had on my life. Although we had only been together for a brief period, his role in my life would carry through my entire adult life. Where my tummy had once experienced beautiful swarms of butterflies, only emptiness remained.

Then there's Ryan; the man of my dreams, trapped in a perpetual game of hide-and-seek with me to this very day. He's amazing in every way and I love him completely, and he, me. It's just . . .

Another Perfect Day

She strolled along the river walk with a casual, carefree stride, although beneath this illusion, a feverish anticipation had amassed that could not get her to her destination quickly enough. The two-mile brick river walk with a long row of oak trees that lined the east side of the walkway, created the perfect amount of shade with its canopy. To the west side of the walkway and about fifteen feet below was the river slowly transporting water to the bay.

Her stroll would always conclude in front of the same park bench. It was her bench, perfectly affixed beneath one of the most gorgeous, sprawling southern oak trees on the walkway, dripping with curtains of grey and light-green Spanish moss. This created a peripheral foreground set of subjects that gave a postcard-perfect perspective to the amazing sunset just beginning to unfold across the river. Not only was this the prettiest bench area, but it also made her feel as if the bench was created exclusively for her. As if at any moment an artist would magically appear to paint her into this surreal postcard.

As she sat, she smoothed the back of her light-red, floral summer dress with both hands in a single graceful motion as she sat, crossing her legs at her ankles.

Somehow she always arrived exactly twenty minutes before each sunset and always just a few moments before his arrival. As he drew closer, she stood to greet him, turning slightly, but not directly toward him. She gently brushed a long lock of her medium brown, loosely curled hair behind her left ear, exposing her entire blushed face to him. A slight warm breeze gently swept through her hair while also kissing her thighs through the bottom of her summer dress. It was by all measures turning out to be another perfect late afternoon.

He was sporting his predictable attire; tight faded blue jeans, a white long sleeve dress shirt with the sleeves slightly rolled up and the top three buttons undone. Those three buttons left undone always got to her, exposing just enough of his broad hairless chest, forcing her to take a deeper breath.

His face, always with a perpetual, well-manicured five o'clock shadow seemed to draw attention to his sandy pink, full lips. Each time he glanced at her, he gave an ever-so-slight yet mysterious upturn toward his left cheek. This expression exposed a sliver of ego mixed with bold yet distinguished confidence that had a pressing agenda.

His eyes were, in a word, dreamy, and of the lightest blue hue. Eyes that, depending on the light, could transform into a mesmerizing deep blue within an instant. The first time he gazed down into her eyes, the unbreakable defensive barrier she spent so long solidifying seemed to melt into oblivion as a thousand little butterflies spontaneously released within her midsection.

In that instant, she stared back into his eyes, refusing to even blink. Her expression was that of an invitation, demanding he take full advantage of her soft lips, designed only for his. At only a tongue's length away, she could feel the warmth of his breath as he parted his lips to help envelop hers. The aromatic undertones of warm mint filled her senses with a deliciousness she was all too ready to taste.

A momentary pause between them caused her breathing to become wonderfully labored as he stole each new breath from her.

Those little butterflies within her midsection had somehow made their way upward to begin a furious frenzy of collisions inside the walls of her heart.

Each encounter stirred uncontrollable excitement within her. It always felt just like their first kiss. It never seemed to get old or mundane, albeit predictable.

She crept her arms up each side of his ribcage, finally coming to rest with her left hand braced upon his right jawline and her right hand draped over his left shoulder. She then leaned in the rest of the way to meet his lips. The taste was even more delicious than she had imagined. His lips, his tongue, his breath complemented the fresh, yet intense, sublime masculine woody aura of his cologne.

His presence and kiss were so intoxicating that her sense of time had completely vanished. It seemed only a single millisecond had passed, yet they were already inside his apartment, continuing where they had just left off at the river walk.

Regardless, his shirt, now of no practical use, came off with a rushed fury, exposing his well-defined chest. He had already gracefully maneuvered her in such a way that her sundress lifted off effortlessly, while simultaneously unfastening and removing her bra in one quick flick of his fingers. This left both his and her skin exposed as each cell of her body begged for its cellular counterpart on his.

Her hands that were busy exploring his midsection, slowly and forcefully moved up to greet his chest. The kissing became more powerful as he grabbed her upper lip with his while falling slowly into a plush, oversized bean bag chair. His lips temporarily retreated from hers to begin further exploration, sending her further and further into an amazing, intoxicating trance.

Staring deeply into his eyes, she softly whispered, "I love you." They had been here so many times. It was like experiencing déjà vu repeatedly. She knew exactly where he would kiss and touch her next.

"Strange?" she thought to herself.

But her question was of no consequence as his energy was too powerful to distract, let alone resist.

The desire in his eyes, deeply intense and focused, revealed what was to come next. This silent and powerful revelation made her quiver as she anticipated what would be the prelude to him passionately and ever-so-delicately working his way snugly inside of her.

Mixed with her passion was also a slight hint of anxiety. She knew now that everything was playing out exactly as it did countless times before. She knew this evening, he would take her virginity. It was so perplexing. They enjoyed intimacy so many times before and yet each encounter brought her back to the same moment she had experienced their first time together.

"How is this happening? I mean, I'm not a virgin. This is the weirdest déjà vu ever."

Just as predicted, she experienced every single feeling associated with their first time together. She could feel the warmth of her wetness being transferred to him as he initially entered. It was a warm, quick pain that rather quickly became an enormous feeling of pressure, soreness, and fullness all at once, as he made his way completely inside. It was at that exact moment she let herself go freely—as all of her senses transformed into a wondrous unbridled passion.

He was so gentle, so delicate, so selfless, and so loving. He never took his eyes off of hers, ensuring he was not hurting her.

Within moments there was no more discomfort, only pleasure. Her back slowly began arching upward. Her toes tightly curled as she gripped the sides of the beanbag chair. Something was starting to happen that was unexpected.

At that very instant, she recalled a conversation with some of her girlfriends telling her she would most likely not climax her first time. "You need to get into your head, you know? It takes a lot of practice and patience, but you'll get there, eventually."

Just before their first interlude had even completed, she felt an intense rush along with a set of rhythmic contractions that momentarily paralyzed her entire body. Waves of incredible pleasure filled her nether as the rest of her tingled with joy. Then with a single, long, soft, and final moan, she became that of a Jell-O mold as he too finished in near unison with her.

The rest of the engagement played out in slow motion as they made love several times over the next four hours. A sheet and comforter already strategically placed next to the beanbag chair allowed him to cover them as he cupped her firmly from behind as they drifted off to sleep.

After what she could easily describe as the best sleep of her life, she awoke to find herself in her bed, in her apartment. The disorientation was dizzying. "Wait. I'm still asleep and only dreaming," she tried to convince herself. But as consciousness slowly took control, she realized what had just occurred was another episode of the recurring dream that had ravaged her so many times before. Strangely, unlike other dreams, this dream would never fade from her memory. In fact, it didn't really feel like a dream at all. It was more like an actual memory, perhaps of a previous life or possibly a second, alternate life.

Although disappointed, she found that it was on those days after the dream she felt the most alive. The dream felt just as real as any of her conscious memories. Like a photograph, every physical detail of him became permanently etched into her memory—his face, his body, his personality, his voice, his scent, his energy, and even his name. Ryan. He followed her everywhere. He haunted her.

"Ryan? Where are you?" she thought.

It was the strangest feeling. The deepest part of her knew she loved him completely, and he, her. She missed him. She missed his eyes, his smile, his aroma. She ached to be with him. This was beyond ordinary. She definitely knew Ryan was real. She was resolute in her convictions, but could not yet put her finger on what was happening.

Switched at Birth?

From the outside, it would seem I was rather content, despite existing as nothing more than the mere shadow of the teenage avatar I occupied. An avatar controlled by an insecure and fearful persona, far too afraid to embrace what I had always known. I was an oxymoron; an ironic result of something gone tragically wrong between heaven and this new life. How could it be that I and this avatar; this shell, were at such odds? How could I and this "boy" coexist within a body that seemed to belong to "him" but everything else, to me?

I always had an innate sense of self. You know, that sense of whom or what you are that usually only lives within your subconscious. That sense of being to which you never gave a recognizable conscious thought. However, my sense of self was annoyingly conscious, perpetually exposed to the cold world like a tooth missing its enamel.

What was most troubling wasn't the recognition that I was different. It was the daily torment it brought; the unforgiving torture of feeling incongruent; and the relentless and bitter awareness that something had gotten completely screwed up during shipping and handling from heaven. It was like realizing you were switched at birth, but instead of being given to the wrong family, you were given to the wrong body.

To clarify, my incongruity wasn't known to me as a feeling. I didn't "feel" like a girl, nor did I "feel" female. I knew I was a girl. I knew I was female. But I have to admit, it was extremely confusing. I knew I was a girl, but everyone else knew and identified me as a boy, a son, a brother, a nephew, and a grandson. It was confusing and frustrating as hell. The confusion I experienced led me to think critically from a young age. I realized that being a girl wasn't an emotion or feeling, but an innate sense of awareness of the person within me.

> **It was like realizing you were switched at birth, but instead of being given to the wrong family, you were given to the wrong body.**

I found myself trapped between two different worlds; between two different aspects of humanity itself. My ever-growing awareness of this conundrum kept me from divulging this revelation to anyone as I would surely be teased, humiliated, and bullied even more than I already was. I knew that unless one had experienced incongruity for themselves, it would be difficult, if not impossible, to fully appreciate the meaning and sheer depth of my struggle. Now, that doesn't mean that when I was a child I had even the foggiest clue what the word *incongruity* meant, but I sensed it within me.

It was arduous. Day after day, year after year, people identified me as a boy while inside I knew I was a girl. Or maybe I was a boy and a girl, if such a thing existed? Or perhaps I was someone with a deformity no one other than myself recognized? Whatever the answer was, even the simple act of looking at myself in the mirror and seeing the wrong person staring back was enough to ruin my entire day all by itself. Perhaps, one of the hardest things to reconcile was the awkwardness of attempting to fit within an identity that felt completely unnatural. It was like being born left-handed (which, coincidently I was) and being forced to only use my right hand for literally everything, no matter how uncomfortable it was.

I studied everyone—my parents, my sister, my cousins, and my friends with the precision of a seasoned private investigator. I needed to know what caused me to be so different from everyone else I knew. While studying, I was becoming more and more aware of the vast yet often subtle differences between boys and girls. I gained a deep sense of knowing. A knowing that told me I had somehow ended up on the wrong team and wearing the wrong uniform. This *knowing* developed far beyond what I could describe as painful, beyond frustrating, and beyond emotional. Every new discovery I made seemed to be deeply rooted in the most primal levels of my humanity. And at that age, I hadn't even begun to understand what humanity even was, let alone all it entailed. All I knew was this would never go away; never leave. Ever.

I wanted so desperately to fit in; to understand and perceive the world just like everyone else. But the complex and frustrating realization that I would never be like everyone else left me feeling less human and over time, increasingly withdrawn. I felt as if I was the only person alive that had to endure life this way. This created an eerie sense of loneliness that had me desperate to push every disturbing thought of my incongruity out of my mind. But accomplishing this proved impossible.

Impossible because my struggle was always the first thought to greet me each morning upon waking, and always the last thought at night before falling asleep. Never a day passed that I did not wish for just a little relief from the relentlessness of it all.

That relief came in tiny snapshots; moments I always looked forward to, where I could be alone. Moments that filled me with a brief yet wonderful sense of excitement and temporary relief. Moments where I could explore my inner self, where I could attempt to feel a little more human, a little more like a whole person.

Learning precisely the time each day when I could be alone for at least a few moments was key. It was during those moments I honed my sneaky skills. Those developing skills ultimately led to me becoming the covert operative I now was. Yes, covert. I needed to keep my time alone private. I somehow sensed that what I was doing was taboo; something that would get me into trouble.

I planned with excruciating detail how every second of my alone time would be spent. This me-time was nearly always carried out in my parents' or sister's bedroom. I studied every detail of both rooms. I knew precisely where to find the exact article of clothing or jewelry I required, its exact placement, and how it was folded or hung. Every borrowed piece of clothing and jewelry was always meticulously placed back exactly as they were found, as if they had never been touched.

With each new day came deeper explorations of closets, dressers, and jewelry boxes. I searched for anything that could help me unveil even the tiniest sliver of who I knew I was. Five minutes here, ten minutes there. It was just never enough time. But those five to ten minutes were, by far, the best part of my day. The painful longing for the life and body I was supposed to have in the first place was temporarily eased.

While I was experiencing temporary moments of relief, the associated isolation inside those moments created their own set of problems. I never had an outlet to express myself with anyone else. There was no sense of affirmation. No sense of sisterhood or friendship that I desired so badly. And no sense of permanency or hope for a magical fix.

Although me-time began just before I turned seven, there were several times since the age of five where I would look at my sister's clothing and dolls and wonder why I could not have the pretty things she had. Why was she allowed to have her hair long, but they forced me to have my hair so short? My sister, Colleen, eighteen months my junior, had an amazing little bedroom, with walls covered with

Holly Hobbie; a cat-loving, rag dress-wearing little girl topped in a gigantic blue bonnet. Complimenting this motif was a beautiful queen-size canopy bed adorned with a semi-transparent white canopy that majestically draped over each side of the bed. I loved my sister's room and wished it was mine.

Me-time officially became a daily routine when Colleen began ballet class. I was only seven years old, and I already held a significant amount of visceral anguish and jealousy. Not Colleen, nor anyone else would ever know or understand the struggle nor the torment I faced knowing I was not permitted to do the same things as her.

Instead, I would be relegated to watch as she practiced at home; absorbing and memorizing every single nuanced move and every technique they taught her. This would, with varying degrees of success and failure, all be reenacted later while I was alone. Slipping on Colleen's stockings, tutu, and slippers gave me a momentary sense of escape and exhilaration as if I was right beside her in ballet class, diligently practicing the same movements again and again until perfected, at least by my standards. Though I didn't know it at the time, Colleen would take ballet for less than a year. But within that year I would study nearly everything she would do and how she would wear that beautiful uniform. A uniform that was eventually neatly packed away in her closet, so I could still at least continue to practice the few movements I had taught myself anytime I wanted. In fact, I did this so often, I would go on to wear her ballet outfit countless more times than Colleen ever had.

Perhaps one of the most memorable and magical parts of me-time involved a pretty jewelry box filled with Mom's necklaces, clip-on earrings, rings, and brooches. When the jewelry box was opened, the most adorable little ballerina stood before me just in front of a small mirror inside the top of the box. I would reach behind the box and wind the knob as the ballerina would to begin to spin to a simple yet beautiful melody.

Hiding From Myself

Mom kept all of her makeup in the bathroom. I knew the real challenge would be applying, then taking it off without getting caught. Instead, I found other ways to fulfill my curiosity. At least once a day, I would use mom's eyelash curler to curl my eyelashes. I'd apply blush and lipstick before taking Mom's large hairbrush to "poof" my horridly short hair, creating lots of body from my already thick mane.

I would look through some of my sister's magazines and study how the girls in the photos applied their makeup. I would flip and flip through the pages until I found someone pretty but not overdone. I understood nothing of what order to apply the makeup, what complexion I was considered, or if my mom or sister even had the right products to accomplish my task at hand. But it was during those years just before puberty, while I was still fairly androgynous, that I had already mastered the application and quick removal of at least some of Mom's makeup products. So I suppose I owe a debt of gratitude to *Tiger Beat* magazine, and Sears and JC Penney's catalogs. I had to use what I had access to, and if one really studies each image carefully, you can learn a great deal.

Now thirteen, and beginning to feel the emergence of puberty, I realized that me-time, to which I had grown accustomed, was about to disappear forever. Instead of catching a glimpse of who I really was, I was instead becoming distressed at the awkward caricature staring back at me in the mirror. When I was younger, I appeared more feminine; more androgynous. But now? Now, I could barely stand to look into that mirror without feeling flawed, awkward, foolish, and increasingly dysphoric. The days of playing dress-up were definitely coming to an end.

The dichotomy that existed within me, along with the lack of understanding of what caused this lifelong struggle, compelled me to believe I had to live two separate lives. Neither capable of providing me with even a modicum of comfort or relief from my struggle. Both denying me an escape from being uncomfortable in my own skin. And both leaving me perpetually suffering in silence.

What remained was my perception of the world looking through two different lenses. It seemed unique and interesting at first. But soon it became utterly exhausting.

I knew how boys talked to each other and what kinds of things they discussed. I also knew how girls talked to each other and the things they would discuss. The differences were striking, and for most I was merely a spectator. The boys talked about things I could not have cared less about. And the girls, well, they never included me in any of their conversations because they considered me a boy.

> **I could barely stand to look into that mirror without feeling flawed, awkward, foolish, and increasingly dysphoric.**

~

I had a completely different idea of what a role model was compared to all the boys in my neighborhood and class. They wanted to grow up to be like Harrison Ford, Sylvester Stallone, Greg Nettles, O. J. Simpson, or Bruce Jenner—I mean, how ironic life can turn out? I, on the other hand, admired while wishing with all of my heart to be as beautiful as Olivia Newton-John, Brooke Shields, or Lynda Carter. Or someone gypsy-like and totally badass like Stevie Nicks or Pat Benatar. But there were two standouts that I identified with far greater than the others.

The first, was Carly Simon. I loved everything about her. Her songs. Her voice. Her look. Her self-confidence. I would later learn that she was a brave, unapologetic feminist who overcame incredible personal adversity, battling her perception of being the youngest sister in her family who was also considered to be an ugly duckling. That part was difficult for me to navigate, especially when speaking to the boys about her.

"Ew. She's weird looking," they'd say. My response was always the same. "I find her very beautiful and unique."

I remember watching her concert on Martha's Vineyard on HBO in 1987, completely mesmerized and wishing I had a front row seat to that show. Martha's Vineyard was a place I was intimately familiar with, as my family would often vacation in Cape Cod during summer breaks. To this day, I still play that concert repeatedly on YouTube.

The other standout, at least for a short while, was Carrie Fisher, Princess Leia in the original *Star Wars* trilogy. She was definitely an independent, beautiful young woman that took charge and didn't take any shit. And bonus, she got to kiss Harrison Ford. Fast forward to today and the same me would identify with actresses like Daisy Ridley who played Rey in the newest *Star Wars* trilogy, Gal Gadot, the newest Wonder Woman, or interestingly, Linda Cardellini from the TV series *Dead to Me*. Then there is my personal favorite, Salma Hayek, who played Isabel in the movie *Fools Rush In*.

As the slow process of puberty unfolded, so did my thoughts about people I found attractive. People I wanted to kiss, and a foreign, yet wonderful new thought. Sex. The kids at school always talked about it, but to be honest, I still did not understand what it really entailed.

I had already had several crushes and knew what it felt like to kiss a girl. Ironically, all of my thoughts and daydreams were of guys. Kissing a girl was fun, but it wasn't very appealing. More appealing were the daydreams where I'd often kiss one of the cute boys from school or TV.

I loved looking at the posters and photos in Colleen's room. Crushing on movie stars or cute boys in school was all so wonderful. But with that came confusion about what my future might hold within the mainstream construct that boys are supposed to be with girls and vice versa.

"How does any of this work?" I thought. "How does a girl with the body of a boy date, let alone get married someday?"

That I found boys attractive only reinforced my truth. I was a girl, and I liked boys. Boys were cute, and that was that. End of story. The only obstacle and barrier to entry to the life I desired was apparently my body. And that would definitely someday be a problem.

At ten years old, I often found myself alone in my sister's bedroom, immersed within the pages of *Tiger Beat magazine*, gazing at the teenage heartthrobs of the 1970s. They were the same guys that girls my age and older found dreamy. Guys like Shaun Cassidy, David Cassidy, Donnie Osmond, Scott Baio, Leif Garrett, John Travolta, Erik Estrada, Robbie Benson, and my favorite, Andy Gibb. Fast-forward to today and they would be in the same league as Jason Momoa, Ryan Reynolds, Tom Hiddleston, Josh Lucas, Jake Gyllenhaal, Idris Elba, Justin Timberlake, Oscar Isaac and of course Chris Hemsworth. I mean, damn! Chris Hemsworth. Okay, sorry.

Anyway, nearly every day, I would flip through the small pile of my sister's magazines daydreaming about what my life would be like if someday one of those celebrities would marry me and have a family. I knew about pregnancy. But embarrassingly, I was painfully unaware even at ten that "getting pregnant" was not in my future. Think this through. I lived in a little Podunk town in upstate New York with more deer than people. The Internet didn't exist yet. There were no smart devices that allowed you to access all the known answers of the universe. Nope. Instead, all I could do was fantasize about being pregnant. When you're born incongruent, all you have are your fantasies and dreams.

But the most memorable look into my identity and orientation was when I went to see the movie, *Grease* with my parents and sister. I found myself totally smitten with and privately in-love with John Travolta; "Danny", while also very attracted to Olivia Newton-John; "Sandy". Danny was amazing. He reminded me of a neighborhood boy down the street I crushed on, albeit with different-colored hair. I wonder now, what that boy would think knowing I had an amazing crush on him throughout my childhood?

But Sandy? Sandy was beyond beautiful. Sandy made me feel "hopelessly devoted" wishing I was her in every way. I loved the way she did her gorgeous blonde hair up with an assortment of cute colored ribbons, or the many gorgeous summer dresses she adorned throughout the movie. And her amazing singing voice and Australian accent absolutely mesmerized me. Although the attraction to her was intense, I somehow knew that Sandy was merely the object of my deepest wishes. She possessed what I did not have. The person I desperately wished I could be, while Danny was my genuine attraction, my veritable crush.

~

At about eleven, I began experimenting with kissing one of the neighborhood girls, Mika. Mika was the prettiest and nicest girl I had ever met. She had beautiful, deep brown eyes that matched her long brown flowing hair. I definitely had a powerful case of puppy love. Although relegated to playing the part of the husband while playing house, Mika and I would kiss for hours nearly every day. We would also write short love letters to each other expressing, in rather simple words, how much we loved one another. What a surreal moment it was when I found those love letters at the bottom of an old box, still legible, while cleaning the attic of my parents' house several decades later.

Each love letter; each kiss, had us playing the same wonderful role in our own versions of our daily fantasy. Unbeknownst to her, we dreamed of and wished for the same things.

But conflicting thoughts would always enter. "Do I like boys and girls? Is Mika my girlfriend or is Mika like Sandy from *Grease*?"

Then, one day, the kissing stopped. Mika walked up to me, and rather matter-of-factly told me she needed to stop kissing me because she was interested in a guy at school named Chris. To me, this was actually comedic. She had been crushing on the same Chris I had been crushing on. Talk about an FML moment. The funny thing was, she never ended up with him. Simultaneously, I would also think, "I wish I was born differently so I could be the one with Chris."

Things were becoming overwhelmingly complex. It was also a time my vocabulary was expanding. I was hearing the words gay and faggot used more frequently from the boys in school.

"If I like boys, does that make me gay or a faggot? How does that work?" I'd anguish.

To make matters even worse, I was becoming increasingly interested in boys.

"Boys are not supposed to like other boys. It's a sin." I recalled.

"But am I really sinning? I can't be. I'm really a girl with a screwed up body. Right?" I argued with myself.

It was the strangest paradox and something to which I had no experience, vocabulary, or context in which to draw upon. Everyone saw me as a boy. Everyone treated me like a boy. So I conceded that maybe I was a boy; a very complicated boy.

> When you're born incongruent, all you have are your fantasies and dreams.

By the summer of age thirteen, things were really starting to come together with my gender identity and sexual orientation. The boys in the neighborhood all gathered to complete the tree fort they had been building for the past month next to Mika's house. They were all fairly skilled at using tools, except me.

"Eddie, you just go get us more 2x4s, we got this," Bob would chuckle.

The other guys included Mika's brother Tom, and the older guy I was crushing on down the road. Watching the boys build were my friend Shannon, Mika, and my sister Colleen.

That guy I had a crush on was busy sawing a piece of wood. He was really into it as I watched him intently.

"Isn't it cool the way his butt swings back and forth when he moves the saw?" I cooed.

Everything came to a complete halt. The "construction crew" immediately turned around with the faces and eyebrows that said, "What did you just say?"

"Fag!" said one of them. Then the rest laughed and chimed in with similar comments.

Shannon looked at me and said, "Oh, my God! You didn't just say that. Do you *want* to get beat up?" she laughed.

The way my brain worked, I didn't see that comment as strange or worthy of the word "fag", but looking at it from their perspectives, I understand why they would have thought so.

Years later in a conversation with Mika's brother, Tom, I reminded him of that day asking him if he recalled that summer, and that comment, in particular.

"Yeah, I remember, but regardless, it never stopped me from hanging out with you," he stated.

"Well, why wouldn't you, it wasn't like I was trying to seduce you?" I responded.

"Now you just hurt my feelings. You weren't attracted to me?" he asked rather disappointedly.

"Really? So you would have kissed me if I tried? I don't think so." I laughed. It's nice to still know some people from my childhood, to relive and laugh at some awkward and special moments.

∼

Each year I dreaded the first day of school, and this year would be difficult for me. I knew that from the very first day of school I would confront the unavoidable observation of changes my girlfriends had been experiencing while on summer break. Physical and emotional changes that would never manifest within me. This was certain to make the eighth grade emotionally exhausting.

An unfamiliar sense of dread and desperation set in. I knew I would have no journey to womanhood. Instead, my journey would comprise an ever-deepening voice, disgusting hair sprouting on my face and body, and an uncontrollable desire to have my fucking lower extremities take over all of my thought processes. Everything was changing in the wrong direction and I was helpless to prevent it, let alone make it magically change direction.

But the greatest comfort was knowing I had someone in my life that provided tremendous comfort. Someone so caring, so empathetic of my internal struggle, that I somehow knew I'd be okay. Someone who would play one of the greatest roles during my younger years attempting to deal with my complex struggle.

A Whispered Prayer

"And lead us not into temptation, but deliver us from evil. Amen."

Each night I'd kneel up against my bed next to Mom while we would recite The Lord's Prayer. After reciting a few other short prayers, Mom would ask me to add my own personal prayer to God. Most nights those personal requests were exactly the same. I would bless Mom, Dad, Colleen, our relatives, and friends. Then, I added one extra request; a wish; a favor that perhaps God could intervene and remedy.

"God? Can you please fix me by morning-time? Amen," I asked sheepishly.

Mom thought it strange that her four-year-old would ask such a thing, so she reached over, put her hand on my little forehead, and asked, "Oh honey, what's broken? Do you feel sick?"

"No."

"But why did you ask God to fix you sweetheart?"

"I feel sad." I cried.

"Oh honey, what's the matter? Tell me what's making you sad."

After a brief pause, I attempted to verbalize the complex thoughts overwhelming my young mind. So I quietly asked, "Mom? Am I a boy *and* a girl?

Mom, seemingly mystified by this odd question, replied, "Honey, you're not a boy and a girl. You're just a boy; my handsome little boy. Why would you say you're a boy and a girl?"

The response I gave was rather simple, "I don't know? I just think I am."

Her physical response to my answer told me she had concerns, but was not angry.

"It's ok," she reassured. "When you're little, life can be a very confusing experience. But I promise you, these feelings will pass. They will go away, and you will be perfectly fine. Okay?"

She then leaned in, kissed me on the forehead, fixed the blankets, and reassured, "I love you. Now go to sleep, okay."

Mom's reassuring words gave me an enormous sense of comfort and relief. After all, she always seemed to have the answers. And at my young age, I certainly wasn't in any position to debate the issue. If Mom says everything's going to be okay, then everything's going to be okay.

Having gained a sense of comfort from hearing my struggle was temporary, I drifted off to sleep. Still, residual discomfort remained from Mom calling me, "her handsome little boy." *That* was a major letdown. I had wished Mom would have told me something different. At that moment I wished I had also told her I wanted to grow up to be as pretty as her. I loved her long, auburn hair. The way she transformed when she put on her makeup mesmerized me. At just four years old, I was studying her intently. I wanted to be like her, much the same way most boys do with their dads.

Although Mom did not understand why her son would think (let alone be distraught over) such things, she responded with a sense of empathy that, looking back, was amazing for a woman that grew up inside of a rigid religious and societal belief system that Western culture had created—the binary. A belief system where your sex and gender are the same. Your genitals define your sex and gender. You can *only* be a boy or a girl; a man or a woman; a male or a female. To this belief system, there was no other option. There was no such thing as a sex or gender spectrum.

Although other cultures of the world had already identified the existence of more than two sexes and genders throughout history, Western culture thought it to be ridiculous. Instead, they placed everyone inside two convenient little containers. This ideology had no room for sexual or gender-based diversity.

As 99 percent of the population would never be at odds with this construct, was it any wonder it became so accepted? Mom would learn no differently. But more than the societal construct, Mom's religion taught her that any deviation from this construct was an abomination to God himself: a sin.

Mom would learn how to make sense of her world through the societal standards of the 1950s, laden with copious amounts of misogyny. It was a continuation of an age-old patriarchal construct, thousands of years in the making.

While she hid them well, she had major issues with the way they viewed women in the 1950s and 60s. I would later come to find that she even had multiple issues with her own religion.

But as a nurse, Mom was already well-versed in how to comfort people, especially if one of those people was her own child. Being a nurse was Mom's gift she bestowed upon countless lives she had attended to. In fact, one of those lives would change the course of her life forever.

⁓

While responding to a structure fire, a local fireman, standing on the back of the fire truck, lost his footing and fell from the moving truck, striking his head on the pavement. This immediately rendered him unconscious. While in a coma, his nurse, Peggy cared for him beyond what her regular rounds required, often sitting and talking to him hoping he would hear her voice and possibly awaken. For the next five days, she continued to talk to him. She took excellent care of this handsome young gentleman, whose misfortune put him where he was. She even took the time to shave his face each day.

On the fifth day, as she was speaking to him, he awakened. Peggy was ecstatic. She quickly informed the doctors of his awakening.

"How are you feeling?" the doctor asked.

"Not so good," he responded.

"Can you tell me your name and birthdate?"

"Bob. September 15th," he quickly replied.

After a few more questions, the doctor examined him. Slowly reaching up to his face, he realized his facial hair was still very short, so he asked, "Doc? Can you tell me what happened last night? I can't remember."

"Well, the first thing you need to know is that last night was five days ago."

Bob was in disbelief until he turned his head to his nurse as she confirmed the doctor's statement with a head nod.

"Bob. This is Peggy. She has been your nurse these past five days. She has taken great care of you and will continue until you are ready to be discharged."

The nurse/patient paradox called the Florence Nightingale effect; a trope where a caregiver, in this case, Peggy, the nurse, and her patient, Bob develop romantic feelings for one another, had taken full effect. Their fateful encounter, during those five days, became a loving marriage of forty-nine years that produced two children. Edward Ambrose (Eddie), assigned male at birth (AMAB), and a younger sister, Colleen Marie, assigned female at birth (AFAB).

A Whispered Prayer

As if being born incongruent wasn't hard enough, by the time I was in kindergarten, I was beginning to quickly lose my hearing. I had become extremely self-conscious and afraid I was going to get in trouble for not being able to hear the teacher, Mrs. Lefkowitz. Everything was a mumble. I could no longer hear words; only murmurings of sounds. I reclused. I found myself not able to communicate with anyone in class. In fact, many of the kids thought I was just ignoring them. During our morning activities, we used to have something called *circle-time*. This consisted of all of the children sitting in a semi-circle around our teacher as she would ask each of us questions. To me it didn't really matter what question she asked, because my answer would always be the same. I would simply nod my head and say the word, "yeah."

It didn't take Mrs. Lefkowitz long to conclude I was experiencing hearing loss. Over the next several months I missed quite a bit of school; even my kindergarten class photo. I went through several diagnostic tests which finally revealed that my eustachian tubes were much narrower than normal and that I could benefit from a couple of surgical procedures in the Children's Hospital in Manhattan. They had revealed to my parents that my hearing was nearly completely interrupted and that these procedures would be necessary to prevent permanent deafness.

I did not learn of this until I was in my early twenties, but I found out that during those procedures, I had an adverse reaction to the anesthesia which required them to resuscitate me.

Just a week later and I was back in school welcoming in a whole new world of sounds. At times, I would cover my ears with my little hands as the sounds overwhelmed my renewed sense of hearing. While it was an adjustment, it was wonderful to be able to hear again. Ironically, I would later grow to become a songwriter, producer, and musician, and unbelievably with perfect pitch.

But along with the wonder of sound, my attention once again shifted. I began to focus once again on the recognition of how different I was. The other kids seemed so oblivious to who or what they were. Yet I was always completely immersed in this dysphoria.

Something as simple as lining up for lunch, the library, or for fire drills was a struggle for me.

"Girls, please line up on the left; boys to the right. And no running," Mrs. Lefkowitz would command.

I would find myself quite often being carefully, and swiftly moved into the "correct" line after making my way to the girls' line. No one really paid attention to my cries. It was the 1970s and I was merely seen as a five-year-old *wiseass*.

~

"God? Can you please fix me by morning-time? Amen."

As time passed, I kept rather quiet and reserved about my struggle. In fact, there were only a few other times during my early childhood that Mom even talked about *it*. Unknown to her, I was praying night after night after night, fruitlessly asking God for the same wish. The anguish was always worse during bedtime. The frustration that God was not intervening and fixing the situation would make me sob, and at eight years old it was already getting old.

"What's wrong, sweetheart?"

"Why doesn't God answer my prayers?"

"What prayers is he not answering?"

"My prayer. To fix me."

Mom, now visibly distraught at the revelation that her son was still praying the same prayer she promised was no longer needed, saw that this was not just a phase as she had first suspected. She thought the issue would simply pass. But it clearly didn't.

Sitting me up in bed, she asked, "This is really still bothering you?"

"Yeah."

A Whispered Prayer

"Do you still think you're a boy and a girl?"

"No. I think like I should be a girl, but I look like a boy. I'm sorry Mom," I mumbled out as I continued to sob.

"Hmm," Mom hugged me while taking a deep breath. "Don't be sorry. I'm not sure I understand what all of this is, but you need to know that you're just a boy, honey. I wish there was something I could say or do to make you feel better. What can I do, sweetheart?"

"I don't know," I replied. "I wish I had things like Colleen. Do you think, just for tonight, I could wear one of her nightgowns?"

She replied, "Boys don't wear nightgowns. But . . . " she paused, then looked into my sister's room. Then in one unexpected movement, she stood up and requested, "Bob, can you throw me one of Colleen's nightgowns? Eddie's pajamas need washing."

Without even giving it a thought, Dad walked the nightgown into my room, handed it to Mom, looked directly at me, then said, with a bit of sarcasm, "Let's not make a habit out of this. Okay?" he softly laughed, exiting the room.

Upon his exit from the room, Mom helped me put on the nightgown. She laid me back down, put her finger to her lips, smiled and whispered, "Shhh. It's okay. Now go to sleep. We'll figure this all out."

Although still frustrated, I felt comforted and thrilled that she let me wear the nightgown to bed. But I was nervous about what Mom might say to Dad about all of this.

Over the next couple of years, Mom did not broach the subject—not once. Now ten years old, it seemed as if she had just discarded the entire issue. It was as if she had completely forgotten about it, or maybe she thought by not focusing on it, it would just eventually go away. If that was her strategy, it was about to be tested very interestingly.

One morning, I stayed home from school because of an earache in my left ear. God, I got earaches more than anyone I knew. Feeling most comfortable resting on the living room loveseat, I wrapped my blanket around me, grabbed a soft pillow, and placed a heating pad up against my aching left ear. The living room was a rather unremarkable, average-sized living room with that loveseat situated kitty-corner about eight feet from the front of the room. In the room's front was a twenty-five-inch console tube TV that weighed more than the damn loveseat. Between the couch and loveseat was Mom's ironing board, along with a heap of Dad's freshly dried dress shirts ready for ironing.

Mom used to love watching soap operas and talk shows. There was a talk show called *The Phil Donahue Show* that she particularly liked. This talk show ran from 1970 until 1996. It featured a lot of interesting people from all walks of life that you don't normally see.

If I had to compare it to a more recent talk show, I suppose it would be a bit of a mashup between Dr. Phil, Oprah, and Kelly Clarkson.

While introducing the show, Mr. Donahue began talking about his guest, a woman from England. A woman that was born and raised, a boy named Barry Cossey. This immediately made my heart flutter and from that moment on, demanded my undivided attention.

Mr. Donohue began showing various photos of Barry when he was a young child. Then he said it; the word that would forever change my personal perspective of *myself*. A word that would help me understand exactly what had plagued me for the past six years.

He announced as if to add shock value, "This person is one of the most talked-about *transsexual* profiles in recent years... She is, Barry, who is now Caroline Cossey, and she is in the United States to talk to *Playboy* about a layout."

From stage left, Caroline emerged, walking gracefully across the stage to her interview chair. She was nothing short of stunning, sophisticated, and tall.

I found myself no longer able to lie down. I sat up as my face felt flush. My excitement was pushing my heart to beat faster and faster while I watched.

A Whispered Prayer

This was the very first time I had ever identified with someone else. "There *is* someone else like me," I thought to myself.

I remember repeatedly glancing towards Mom to ensure she did not notice the sheer exhilaration I was experiencing. After a few glances, Mom looked back at me and said, "Is this like your fix me prayer?" She paused as I nodded in agreement. "Okay, let's see what this is all about."

Mom and I continued to watch the rest of the show until, at least for her, her daily call with her best friend, Vivian prevented it. So I watched the rest of the show by myself.

Transsexual. I needed to know more about this word—this unfamiliar word that could describe and identify me for the very first time. Was this word in the encyclopedia? With Mom busy on the phone in the kitchen, I immediately made my way to our collection of encyclopedias. I began skimming the covers to find the volume containing words beginning with "t". I flipped through nearly all the pages with exhausting fervor, but to no avail. I tried many other words that might mean the same thing, but also to no avail.

Mom had just finished her phone call and came back into the room. "Why would you do this to me?" she exclaimed rather unexpectedly. She then cried.

It would be several days before I would get back to those encyclopedias to continue my search. That's when I happened upon a book hidden behind the encyclopedias. It was a hardcover book with black lettering on the cover that said, *Everything You Always Wanted to Know About Sex* (*But Were Afraid to Ask)—explained by David Reuben, M.D.*

Jackpot! I'd definitely find the word transsexual inside this book. I skimmed through the 340+ page book, page by page. Just as I was ready to give up I finally found the word. It was in one of the last chapters of the book, but there it was. Three entire pages dedicated to the discovery of who I was and how to get there from here. Not

23

only did it describe what a transsexual was, but it talked about hormones. It described the specific surgeries needed to turn a penis into a vagina and where it could be done— in Bangkok, Thailand. It also described breast augmentation. It was a lot to absorb.

If only I read this way in school, I could have been a solid A student. I read every word meticulously, trying to absorb every word, every letter on those pages. It became habitual as I would read those same pages nearly every day. I quickly realized I needed more information.

One advantage of growing up in a small town in the 1970s and 80s was having the ability to walk downtown without fear. Kids could go pretty much wherever they wanted, so long as they told their parents and were home by dinner or sundown; whichever came first.

It was just under one mile to the public library. With my library card in hand, I was more than ready to find out more about transsexuals. But I wondered if a small-town library would have such information? So instead of trying to explain to the librarian why I needed to requisition such a book from a larger regional library, I took a fresh approach. I began searching for anything on Thailand and its people, recalling several paragraphs in the book at home mentioning sex change surgeries in Bangkok, Thailand.

It described them as Kathoey, which in English means ladyboy, but in wider references, it included men that were gay and people that were intersex.

Out of only three books related to Thai culture, I found only one with an entire chapter devoted to Kathoey, or the third gender.

"Third gender?" I asked myself. "There are people that don't fit into male or female. Wow."

It described a branch of Buddhism practiced in Thailand called Theravada Buddhism in which there are four genders, not only male and female but also bhatobyanjuanaka and pandaka.

There was also reference to a relatively new word used in the West called transgender. Shocked that this tiny small-town library even

A Whispered Prayer

had a book that mentioned transgender people, I excitedly moved on and began cross-referencing the words transgender and intersex. After scouting several other sources, I finally found a definition for transgender, but nothing for intersex.

The word "transgender" is an umbrella term that describes those who have a gender that's different from the sex assigned at birth: male or female.

What I managed to find then was another unfamiliar word—hermaphrodite. After a little more digging I found that the word intersex was a replacement of the older term, hermaphrodite. I wrote out all the new terms and definitions into my journal.

In the book on Thai culture, it further defined what a sex change entailed. There were hormones, introducing estrogen, and the blocking of testosterone. Various surgeries. Surgeries that allowed people to be congruent. I was utterly riveted.

The library was about to close which left me frustrated that I had to leave. But, on the good side, I was quickly developing a new and foreign vocabulary. Terms that I bet no one else in my tiny town even knew existed. The sex change seemed to be the key to fixing all of my struggles. The burning within my stomach told me I needed to have this done! But Bangkok was on the other side of the world.

~

Five years later, and still relying on the local library for information, I was now becoming very familiar with microfiche articles concerning everything from violent crimes committed against transsexuals to short news stories that covered many pride events around the country.

"Hi, Mom and Dad. I need a passport so I can run away from home and get a sex change in Bangkok."

But possibly the biggest find was several travel advertisements showing vacation packages to Thailand. But to be honest, seeing this raised more questions than it answered.

I was in a good position for someone my age. I had amassed over $4,000 working on a local dairy farm over the past two summers. I asked the librarian, "How does someone get to Bangkok, Thailand and how do I find information on that?"

"Now, why would a young man like you need to know that?"

"It's for a school project. I need to show how someone would travel there."

"I see. I'm not sure any of these books will help you with that. But maybe your parents can help you get in touch with a travel agent for that kind of information. You've got to consider passports, airline tickets, a twenty-two-hour flight, hotel reservations, dining, and you would probably need the guidance of an experienced person who was already well-traveled in Thailand."

The librarian's information was all I needed to realize that going to Bangkok anytime soon would be impossible. I had no passport. I couldn't ask my parents to get me one. I mean, what would I even say?

"Hi, Mom and Dad. I need a passport so I can run away from home and get a sex change in Bangkok."

I'd hear the conversation playing back in my mind in all of its ridiculousness.

It was ludicrous. Although my parents loved me completely, I knew that moving along that timeline would have me in a mental hospital—fast.

With Bangkok wiped out in a single conversation, I dug further and further into medical journals and to my amazement, found several surgeons in the United States that performed these surgeries. I also found that the sex-change surgery had become known as Sex Reassignment Surgery (SRS).

I had a new thumbtack to place on the map in my room. Trinidad, Colorado. a rather small town, not much different from my own. A town of fewer than ten thousand people. Known as the sex change capital of the U.S., Trinidad would be far easier to get to, and as a bonus, it required no passport to get there.

I was able to learn a lot more about how it all works, now that I had a resource relatively close to home. Details explaining the surgery, how much it cost, all about hormones. There was a famous surgeon named Stanley Biber who performed the surgeries. He followed a protocol called the Harry Benjamin Standards of Care. This protocol was basically a consensus opinion on transsexual treatment by medical and psychological experts. There were various scenarios listed in the document which outlined what they considered the appropriate methods to implement when treating someone with *transsexualism*. It seemed their preferred sequence involved administration of hormones, then living as a woman for at least one year before any surgery could be considered. Making things far more complex for me to understand was the idea that they also considered appropriate the opposite order; living as a woman for at least one year (*real life experience*) *before* the administration of hormones. Although I didn't understand much yet, I knew the latter of the two seemed like a stupid idea.

"Why would they want someone, who has all masculine features, to put themselves in danger, while causing incredible discomfort for that same individual?" I stewed. To me, even at this point in my life, I thought these *experts* were actually making this shit up as they went along. To me, they understood very little themselves. We were just a learning process during experiments.

> I also recognized that the Standards of Care was nothing more than a gatekeeping document to prevent liability for something they still didn't understand.

While I understood to a point that they were attempting to protect certain individuals—apparently, from themselves—I also recognized that the Standards of Care was nothing more than a gatekeeping document to prevent liability for something they still didn't understand.

It was getting frustratingly complex and disheartening. There were brick walls everywhere. "Why?" I cried. "Why are there all of these illogical rules?"

As I moved on, I began studying a book called the *Diagnostic and Statistical Manual of Mental Disorders*; the *DSM*; in particular, the *DSM-III*. According to the *DSM*, I found that I was most likely suffering from a mental illness called, "Gender Identity Disorder." There it was in black and white. Just as I had suspected all along, it described me as having a mental health issue. Now there was no way I would ever tell anyone of my lifelong struggle. Maybe that's why the Harry Benjamin Standards of Care exists?

This new information would have to remain inside; quietly hidden away. My deepest, most painful secret would most likely have to go to the grave with me. While detesting the emerging idea forming in my head, I knew I would have to do whatever it took to be a *guy* and do *guy* things. I wish I had the courage to tell my mom straight away that I was *not* going through a phase. But every time I gained the courage to tell her, I backed away. I didn't want to risk having her become angry rather than the supportive Mom she had been since I was four. My irrational fear grew stronger and stronger with each passing day that I didn't come out completely.

That night I would write more pages in my journal than any other night. I had been making entries over the past eight years. I knew there would be a temporary reprieve from my pain while I wrote out my feelings. What I didn't know was that what I had just learned and penned would become a game-changer with lifelong consequences and triumphs. But tagging along with those feelings were disturbing questions. Maybe all of this fear is because I'm a sinner? Maybe I'm insane? Those questions were imprinted into the deepest part of my persona and stemmed from a disturbing lecture I received from one of my older aunts when I was only nine years old.

Losing My Religion

Mom's side of the family lived in a small hamlet in northeastern Pennsylvania and nearly every weekend, we would travel to see them. As kids, we really loved going there. But as time passed, it became a place, at least for me, that being Catholic took on a whole new and frightening meaning.

One of my great aunts, while mostly a caring and independent woman, was one of the more outspoken of my Catholic relatives. One day she gave an especially graphic and bitterly disturbing brief lecture on gay people and other people called *trannies*.

"They're all perverted, dangerous child molesters!" she preached. "The lot of them are disgusting, abominations to God. They are sinners sent by the devil to trick and steal the morality from the innocent. People like them will burn in Hell for all eternity. So if you ever see one, stay away from them."

I have to say, those few sentences scared the shit out of me. She then moved in closer and in a quiet whisper, warned, "I wish you didn't live in New York. You shouldn't have to live out there. You need to be so very careful cause them gay blacks 'il rape you."

At nine years old, I didn't yet understand the sickness that infected every word she had just spoken. But, I had already recognized how different I was and that made her words resonate viciously within me. I knew she had been describing some gross, mythological caricature of *me*.

> "Am I going to Hell? I don't want to go to Hell!"

"Child molesters? Mentally sick abominations?" I worried. I don't want to be one of those.

Within seconds I developed a sense that I was guilty of numerous mortal sins as defined by my aunt's interpretation of our shared religion. Not only was I a girl in a boy's body, which by all Catholic measures was an abomination, but I was also guilty of already being hopelessly attracted to boys, which, as I understood it, was apparently the work of the devil himself.

This went far beyond any conversation I had ever experienced and well beyond my capability to handle another single word. Shaken, I excused myself to the bathroom, shut and locked the door before collapsing to the floor next to the bathtub, hugging my knees, and crying.

"Am I going to Hell? I don't want to go to Hell!" I cried. "God? Why am I like this? What's wrong with me?"

Looking back, all I can say was she was one hell of a racist homophobe, and apparently, painfully unaware of it. I began noticing how some of my other relatives would refer to people. They'd use phrases like *"them gays"* or when speaking about people of color as *"them blacks."* There was a powerful sense of us vs. them built into their vocabulary. It turns out their little quaint town of about 5,000 people comprised a demographic of 99 percent white Catholic and a few other Christian and Jewish denominations.

They all seemed genuine and friendly except when it came to diversity. Many of them seemed profoundly lost within their own religious ideologies and mythologies. And worse, they were unaware of their biased diatribe against unfamiliar forms of the human condition. To this day, many of those very people; relatives included, would dismiss such an outrageous accusation of anyone in the family ever having such a biased view. But that is what I learned from that place when I was a child.

Most of my aunts, uncles, and cousins are not as religiously biased as previous generations were so many years ago and that goes for all of my relatives, not just those in Pennsylvania. But sadly, many remain profoundly lost in between their tired religious ideology and medical science. The criticisms I've heard include, "I love you, but I don't agree with it", "You realize you are sinning against God, don't you?", and "You need to come back to Christ." Then there were downright selfish and hurtful comments by a few of them. "I will never call you by your new name. That is NOT who you are! And you never will be." Yeah, that conversation was a hoot.

I was so excited to share my story with each of my relatives. It's too bad many of them took the position they did. They don't understand what this is, and sadly, they don't want to understand. That is the definition of blind faith or willful ignorance. They can't fathom that I have struggled since I was four. They see what they see. They too often judge a book by its cover. No matter what it's called, to me it remains a painful scar.

They use scripture that they themselves have never read nor seen outside of the church as a justification for questioning my humanity. They never did understand that my humanity has never been up for debate. I am an example of the vast diversity that exists within the human condition. The diversity we see every single day. But certain Catholics and Christians shit a cow if gender or sex is within that diversity.

Before we go too far, let me state that if you follow a religion, I am not here to bash religion into the ground. I simply wish to illustrate the vast difference between religion and spirituality. Religion, at least for now, still serves a purpose. So as you read, understand that from my vantage point, religion is the causality for countless homicides, assaults, bullying, and other terrible things within my demographic. And all in the name of God or Jesus. Why? Because someone said it was so, therefore it must be so.

As an individual raised Catholic, I know intimately that most Catholics don't actually read the bible. Sure, they'll say the Rosary and other prayers, but, the bible, "Let's save that for Sunday mass." In fact, a study conducted by the Pew Research Center found that over 73 percent of Catholics do not read the bible regularly, or at all. And when you've read as many religious texts as I have, you notice that all of them have one thing in common. Gifted authors, but men nonetheless wrote them.

The reality is (and to the chagrin of many a Catholic) there were many writings being reviewed and considered in the New Testament. It was the Church that ultimately decided which books and writings made it to the last version of what we now call the New Testament. *Record scratch* Okay—hold the phone. For my entire life, I had been told the bible was the instruction manual for all of humanity; inspired and written by God. But man edited and censored it? As a matter of fact, yes.

In the year AD 325, over three centuries after Jesus lived, Constantine the Great called the First Council of Nicea. The council was composed of over 300 religious leaders, each charged with the decision to include or exclude the many books and various writings that would make it into the final draft of the Bible. Interesting. You'd think, God, who is omniscient and omnipotent would have that task all locked up.

I think it's important to think about the rationale and theological logic that was driving the early Church for one moment by giving some examples of how belief systems can affect rational judgment. From the days of the Old Testament and continuing well through the age of the New Testament, leprosy; what we now know to be a chronic mycobacterial infection of the skin and nerves, had a long biblical history of being demonized. The terms "leprosy" and "leper" were considered a punishment for sinful behavior— by one's own hand, or by one's parents'. They perpetuated these terms along with their wildly inaccurate description of this most unfortunate disease until the twentieth century. In fact, the tide did not change until modern-day Christian missions pioneered a new position on this age-old disease through the use of sympathy and compassion. They finally replaced this long and widely held view and unnerving bias that defined a leper as someone who is unclean and stricken by God. They replaced it with a scientific definition from the discovery made by a Norwegian physician, G.H. Armauer Hansen in 1873.

Although my arguments may sound harsh, not this chapter nor this book is attempting to convince people to abandon their faith, but to give historical context. In fact, many people from many religions are empathetic, loving, and caring people. The points I am bringing up are for those that don't know of the dangerous and violent content of the books they say they read. This is for those that conclude what God says we must follow and need a serious wake-up call.

There are countless examples of the religious declaring and/or describing something they don't comprehend as ethereal, or paranormal. "It must be the work of the devil or demonic forces."

Let's look at how most religions and their respective followers have strayed from many old teachings and commandments within the various versions of the bible. It would be remiss not to consider these often violent and dehumanizing passages from both the Old and New Testaments.

"You may purchase male or female slaves from among the foreigners who live among you. You may also purchase the children of such resident foreigners, including those who have been born in your land. You may treat them as your property, passing them on to your children as a permanent inheritance. You may treat your slaves like this, but the people of Israel, your relatives, must never be treated this way." Leviticus 25:44–46 NLT

"Slaves, obey your earthly masters with deep respect and fear. Serve them sincerely as you would serve Christ." Ephesians 6:5 NLT

"If a man have a stubborn and rebellious son, which will not obey the voice of his father, or the voice of his mother, and that, when they have chastened him, will not hearken unto them: Then shall his father and his mother lay hold on him, and bring him out unto the elders of his city, and unto the gate of his place; And they shall say unto the elders of his city, This our son is stubborn and rebellious, he will not obey our voice; he is a glutton, and a drunkard. And all the men of his city shall stone him with stones, that he die." Deuteronomy 21:18–21

"He that is wounded in the stones, or hath his privy member cut off, shall not enter into the congregation of the Lord." Deuteronomy 23:1 NRSV

"But if this thing be true, and the tokens of virginity be not found for the damsel: Then they shall bring out the damsel to the door of her father's house, and the men of her city shall stone her with stones that she die: because she hath wrought folly in Israel, to play the whore in her father's house: so shalt thou put evil away from among you." Deuteronomy 22:20–21

"If in spite of this you still do not listen to me but continue to be hostile toward me, then in my anger I will be hostile toward you, and I myself will punish you for your sins seven times over. You will eat the flesh of your sons and the flesh of your daughters." Leviticus 26:27–30

Talk about misogyny! *"I permit no woman to teach or have authority over men; she is to keep silent." Timothy 2:11*

"For every one that curseth his father or his mother shall be surely put to death: he hath cursed his father or his mother; his blood shall be upon him." Leviticus 20:9

"And if thy hand offend thee, cut it off: it is better for thee to enter into life maimed, than having two hands to go into hell, into the fire that never shall be quenched." Mark 9:43

According to Matthew, God is apparently a narcissist as well.

"For I am come to set a man at variance against his father, and the daughter against her mother, and the daughter in law against her mother in law. And a man's foes shall be they of his own household. He that loveth father or mother more than me is not worthy of me: and he that loveth son or daughter more than me is not worthy of me." Matthew 10:35–27

"Anyone who blasphemes the name of the Lord is to be put to death. The entire assembly must stone them. Whether foreigner or native-born, when they blaspheme the Name they are to be put to death." Leviticus 24:16 NIV

> *"Observe the Sabbath, because it is holy to you. Anyone who desecrates it is to be put to death; those who do any work on that day must be cut off from their people." Exodus 31:14*

Another violent failure to understand how sexual orientation works.

> *"If a man has sexual relations with a man as one does with a woman, both of them have done what is detestable. They are to be put to death; their blood will be on their own heads." Leviticus 10:13*

Not sure I'd have any friends left on this one.

> *"If a man has sexual relations with a woman during her monthly period, he has exposed the source of her flow, and she has also uncovered it. Both of them are to be cut off from their people." Leviticus 10:18*

To be sure, I could list dozens of pages of scripture that have pitted man against man; told them to commit terrible atrocities in the name of "the chosen." Biblical rules that are crystal clear what the punishment is for disobeying them. Scores of rules that the vast majority within society no longer follow. The religious along with their respective institutions seem to cherry-pick what they want or don't want to follow. Unfortunately, exceptions are kept in place for things to which they do not understand—or worse yet, do not want to understand.

Let's be clear. There is nothing in the Bible that even comes remotely close to talking about, let alone suggesting anything about individuals that are transgender. With that said, it does not stop the willfully ignorant from making their own interpretations of something you think God would be "dog-shit clear about" especially if it is considered such an abomination. Again, mythology gets reborn over and over throughout the ages, and always with a new foe.

Consider this verse from Deuteronomy, which is often used as an argument against transgender people.

"A woman must not wear men's clothing, nor a man wear women's clothing, for the Lord your God detests anyone who does this." Deuteronomy 22:5

There are many things that make this widely misinterpreted verse in the Bible invalid. You'd think God himself was a jokester and purposely placed riddles in the Bible just to fuck with us. In no particular order, here they are.

This verse clearly talks about cross-dressing. Cross-dressing is not synonymous with being transgender. In fact, if you truly want to get technical, when I assimilated and unnaturally conformed to living as a man, I was actually cross-dressing by wearing casual business attire for men. If this verse is to be held true, then there should be millions of women who should be considered abominations for wearing their boyfriend's shirt or other pieces of clothing she borrows from him. We should consider the simple act of a man placing his jacket around his girlfriend is grounds for God, himself, detesting her.

Other verses commonly misused in a vain attempt to condemn people that are transgender can be found in the book of Genesis by taking the word "and" and making it binary, when, in fact, we see the use of this word to encompass a broad spectrum.

*"In the beginning God created the heavens **and** the earth." Genesis 1:1*

We see this illustrated very clearly above as all Christians interpret and accept that God created not just the heavens *and* the ground beneath, but everything in between.

> *"I am the Alpha **and** the Omega," says the Lord God, "who is, and who was, and who is to come, the Almighty."*

As illustrated above, again the word *and* is used as a broad-spectrum rather than the binary. God is not only the Alpha, and only the Omega. God is, as stated in the verse above, everything in between.

> *"So God created mankind in his own image, in the image of God he created them; male **and** female he created them."*

Nowhere in the bible does it refer to sex and gender, which we all hopefully know are two distinct things. The decision to convert the meaning of the word *and* from "a broad spectrum; all-encompassing" to "binary; only this and only that" is an interpretive assumption that is not based in reality, but based in rudimentary and outdated observation. Instead, this becomes the foundational assumption used to interpret something that is unwritten. To state there is only male and female is to say there is and never has been any variation.

As a simple example, what of people that are intersex? The only word in the bible that they can run to is "eunuch," which is a man that has been castrated. This has absolutely nothing to do with intersex individuals born with any of several variations in sex characteristics, often producing various combinations of genitalia and other reproductive organs from both sexes. But it is even far more complex than that.

Another common argument is that DNA and DNA alone makes us who we are. Regardless of the paradoxical aspects of that point, it begs another question. What was their argument before we discovered the double helix in the 1950s or when we finally completed the human genome in April 2003? Interestingly, the same people who defame medical science many times use medical science in their argument.

This all points to something within a society that goes far beyond being willfully ignorant and just plain uneducated. It speaks to a rigid bias within the basic tenets of their belief systems, which have no empirical evidence to support their claims because their *truth* is predicated on faith and faith alone.

That they use these as arguments even defy theological concessions and observations throughout history where the Church conceded they had it wrong. These are things the devout do not want to know. Regardless, they have been studied and documented extensively by the medical science, psychological, and theological communities.

⁓

Okay, so where did I leave off? Right. I was crying in the bathroom at Grandma's house. A few moments later, I emerged from the bathroom, tears completely wiped away; ensuring to everyone I was ok. I returned just in time to see Grandma gathering the rest of the grandkids together for prayer time.

Grandma was more reserved and softly-spoken, avoiding the types of conversations I had with my great aunt just moments ago. Instead, Grandma would stress the importance of reciting prayers every day. To ensure success in this endeavor, she would place all the grandchildren on the living room couch and tell each of us to turn around to look at the large rectangular picture of a close-up of Jesus of Nazareth standing in front of a backdrop of Jerusalem. After having us recite all of our prayers, Grandma would carefully shake the picture. To our amazement, several pieces of chocolate would fall from behind the picture onto the couch. Because of who I was and because I was the eldest of the cousins, I paid attention to things my other cousins didn't. I had quickly surmised that Grandma was finding creative ways to make us pray.

"I saw what you did right there, Gram," I whispered. "You're good."

I could tell Mom's persona came from Grandma. In fact, to be honest, most memories of my Pennsylvania-based relatives are very fond.

Thankfully, growing up Catholic within my home was not as OCD, nor did it resemble anything close to what I encountered in Pennsylvania. Back in New York, I attended CCD; a one-hour religious studies class each Sunday morning at nine o'clock, and mass at 10:15. Then there were the nightly prayers at bedtime. But that was it. There were no boring lectures about church doctrine and dogma. And no scary mythological stories about Hell and the devil.

The interpretive religious differences between my family and our relatives gave me solace. I felt blessed to have been born to *my* parents. Other than my struggle, I really had a wonderful family filled with love and devoid of visible conflict. Even during a time when there was no detailed nomenclature or vast centralized knowledge base I could draw upon to get simple definitions and answers. All I had was this unfinished portrait of me, a girl, but also a boy. Without understanding my feelings and thoughts, I was experiencing tremendous self-induced dissonance about what I was and who I was. I didn't even have a proper name.

A Rose by Any Other Name

Newsflash. No—we don't like being asked where we came up with our *new* name. And hell to the no—we don't like being asked what our name used to be. Okay? Savvy? ¿entiende? However, *I am* going to tell you, just to get under my own skin for a few minutes.

For as long as I can remember, I have always been creative. I had been pretending I was just an ordinary girl during my moments alone, for quite some time. As strange as it sounds, as I would play with Colleen's dolls, I would wish that their long flowing blonde hair could magically become mine. Sometimes my wishes would even go as far as pretending aliens had abducted me. When they learned of my conundrum, they used their advanced technology to transform me into the girl I was meant to be. Not because I had just seen *Close Encounters of the Third Kind*, but because of the time I had spent developing my imagination. I needed it to help mitigate the frustration and dysphoria I felt every single day.

"I'm a girl inside of a boy!"

God was obviously not the answer to my struggle, so eventually, I would cease asking God to fix me. Instead, my new prayer to God was to make my incongruity disappear; to kill the relentless, innate sense within me that screamed, "I'm a girl inside of a boy!"

I also became enamored with words. I began to write very simple short stories and soon asked Mom and Dad if I could have a typewriter. Although only eight years old, I had amassed a rather sizeable collection of short stories. It was also during this time that I discovered how therapeutic it was to write down my feelings. This discovery began what would later become my life's journal. Nearly every chance I got, I would add entries into my journals, which at the time comprised pages and pages of loose-leaf paper. To ensure no one would find my secret journals, I folded and taped the pages underneath the bottom of my dresser.

Other than stories, I would . . . well, I would write myself love letters. Okay, yes, that sounds really pathetic on the surface, but those love letters were extensions of myself holding on to hope that I would someday find *my own Prince Charming*. I would close my eyes and think of him. I knew what he looked like and knew how he spoke to me. He would court me by writing short love letters and sonnets to win me over. I would pen these love letters and poems, not of my hand, but of his, for the next several decades of my life. Amazingly, I kept every last one of them safe and sound, and still have them all these years later. It became a surreal lifelong romance that defined the truest love I had ever known.

⁓

I always disliked my name. Edward! And just to sprinkle a little more awkwardness onto the situation, my middle name was Ambrose! Ambrose? No one has a middle name like that! Okay. My grandfather's name was Ambrose, but my dad said no one ever called him by that. They called him Slim; his lifelong nickname because he was so thin. Sadly, I never met him as he passed the year before I was born.

A Rose by Any Other Name

Given the angst I had for my given name, I found consolation in the fact that no one ever called me Edward. Instead, I was always referred to as Eddie. I was okay with Eddie. It seemed softer and less bold than Edward. Edward, at least in my mind, brought forward images of a wealthy fair-skinned Englishman and a far cry from who I knew I really was.

There had to be another name I could have? I needed a proper name that matched who I was. I needed a proper salutation in each of *his* love letters; both on the envelope and within each salutation. I thought of every beautiful girl's name I could. But none of them "fit." They just meant nothing to me.

It was during one of my *find a new name sessions*, that I wrote out my complete given name. Eddie Ambrose Washington. As I spelled it out, magically, my middle name isolated itself from the rest of the name and transformed into something beautiful right before my eyes.

I wrote out the letters, one by one. A - m - b - r - o - s - e. After only one iteration, I had rewritten it as, A - m - b - e - r R - o - s - e. It was as if the name had already been divinely seeded and revealed at this precise moment in my life. I now had a name written out right in front of me that made sense. It fit. After lamenting for so long over my name, I had, within a few minutes, changed it and its meaning forever. I could finally visualize the salutations which would appear on each of the letters, "My Dearest Amber Rose, . . ."

"Amber Rose Washington. That sounds pretty. But what's Amber?" I thought.

I made my way downstairs to our set of encyclopedias to see if Amber was even an actual word. Personally, I had never heard of it before. But there it was—Amber, along with pictures of beautiful, shiny, yellowish-brown beads. According to the definition, Amber was a fossil resin valued for its beauty, that had been used to create jewelry since ancient times.

That was it. I had my name. And I secretly had the benefit of having Mom's middle name, Rose. It seemed very fitting to me since

Hiding From Myself

she was, or at least I thought she was, the only person who knew of my struggle.

From the age of eight onward, not only was I a girl but my name was Amber Rose Washington. The only problem was that it would have to, at least for now, remain another secret.

Prelude to a Kiss

"Eddie, you're going to miss the bus. Now get a move on!" It had been the third time Mom attempted to wake me.

Finally managing to reach the sitting position on my bed, I managed, in an almost indiscernible yet agitated pubescent mumble, "Okay Mom, I'm up."

Waking was easy. Harder was the daily task that required the use of the bathroom mirror. That goddamned mirror! It was constantly reflecting the wrong person back at me. Each look into it compelled me to gaze upward beyond the plaster bathroom ceiling and cry out under my breath, "Ugh, Fuck!! Seriously God?" And with each new day, this observation grew more obvious and painful. The toxic chemicals invading my soft and still androgynous body were on a mission to deform me in ways that I could only describe as horrifyingly grotesque.

So there I was, already emotionally exhausted, and it was only 7:15 a.m.

"Come over here and let me fix your hair." Mom attempted to run a straight comb through my thick auburn hair to no avail. "Wow. Your hair is so thick and getting long. We need to get you a haircut."

"No. I like it longer, Mom. You know?" I was giving her the look one gives when silently trying to convey, *you know what I mean*?

With a puzzled look of concern, Mom, using only her eyes, replied with a single word. "Still?"

"Yeah," as I walked away from her.

So there I was, Eddie; Amber, a rather drab, shy, and invisible thirteen-year-old ready for yet another day of torment at school. Each day, trying to fit in with anyone, anyway I could.

> That goddamned mirror! It was constantly reflecting the wrong person back at me.

If you want to get a sense of how different cliques magically formed, then lunch was definitely the place to see it in action. The students were self-segregated into a few different cliques. There were those dedicated to the average, ordinary followers. There were the pretentious, "I'm all that" girls' tables that had a waiting list for future seating. Two popular guys' tables; one comprising your typical country boys and the other comprising the jocks and extroverts. Last but not least, there were those set aside for the smart, nerdy kids. The entire cafeteria was a scene straight out of any high school movie.

Most enjoyable was watching the spectacle of students rushing to the popular tables, attempting to squeeze just one more person into an already over-capacity table. They were obviously uncomfortable, but once squeezed in, well, they were *in*.

I didn't really belong to any one group or clique. I kind of felt somewhat associated and dissociated with them all at the same time. I could sit at just about every different cliquey table without a problem. This was kind of fun, because I would hear the jocks make fun of the nerdy kids—but ironically, the nerdy kids made fun of the jocks far more often.

I wasn't an outcast by any measure. Although I was shy, I was well-liked by others from several cliques. There were several days I would end up at the popular guys' table: the jocks and extroverts. I sat down next to Aaron, who was quickly becoming one of the more popular guys in school. Let's just say, sitting near him was nice.

"Hey, what are you doing after school today?"

"Me? Nothing."

"You think you can come over to my house? I know it's like a mile or so. Bring your bike or something. I want you to hear something crazy from a record I just got."

"Okay, I'll come over after checking in with Mom."

Besides Chris, Aaron was by far one of the cutest guys in my class. He was amazingly handsome and confident, with a smile and demeanor that could convince any girl, within a second, to go out with him. Getting an invitation from him was exciting and unnerving. While incredibly attracted to him, I knew nothing would ever become of that attraction. It was another one of those many crushes that would stay private, like my *real name*.

That day, I went home and washed, brushed my hair in a frenzy, and put on some clothes I thought were flattering. I brushed my teeth, dabbed on an almost unnoticeable amount of Mom's perfume. Then I grabbed some Tic Tacs and while walking out the front door told Mom I was going to walk across town to Aaron's house.

His house was amazing. It was three stories tall. The yard was gigantic and fenced off. They had two horses grazing in the adjacent field. I knocked on what appeared to be their kitchen door. Aaron's mom answered. She seemed somewhat unwelcoming. I was taken back by her face, which had a hint of long-term unhappiness ingrained into it.

"Hi Ma'am. Is Aaron here?"

"He's upstairs. What's your name?" as she opened the door.

"Eddie Washington. I live across town over on Hope Street."

I got the feeling she was not very personable. "Okay, come in." Then she shouted, "Aaron, you have company."

"Okay. Eddie, come on up."

"Go ahead. He's in his bedroom upstairs."

I thanked her and began walking up the stairs.

I saw Aaron standing in the hallway gesturing to me to hurry. I walked into his bedroom as he flashed a vinyl record at me and said, "Sit on the bed. Dude, you're not going to believe this."

"Ick. He called me dude." I reflected. Things were already becoming dysphoric. He turned on his record player and began playing the vinyl record. Yeah, um, if you don't know what that is, Google it.

"What group is this?" I asked.

"What? Led Zeppelin man. Don't you know Led Zeppelin?"

"Um. No."

"How do you *not* know Led Zeppelin? Wow, you *definitely* need to get out more. 'Stairway to Heaven' is one of the best songs ever recorded. Let's listen to it first, then I'm going to freak you out and play it backward. Wait till you hear! You're going to freak, man!"

He started the song and sat down right next to me on the bed as we listened to this song I'd never heard before. He was sitting very close to me, which caused me a bit of difficulty focusing 100 percent on the song. My pulse was racing. I was sitting on the bed of one of the cutest, most popular guys from school, not to mention I was already crushing on him.

When the song finished, he played it backwards so we could hear a ghostly voice sort of saying the words, "Here's to my sweet Satan" and "There's no escaping it."

"Wow! That's creepy!" as goosebumps overtook my body. "I don't think I want to hear that ever again." It really was creepy.

Aaron knew he totally freaked me out, so he instead put on another new song called "Urgent" from a record called Foreigner 4.

I knew this one and liked it. "Now this I know."

Aaron sat next to me again. He gave me a little nudge with his shoulder, looked at me, and said, "I told you I'd freak you out."

As I looked back at him, it seemed, at least for a brief second, our eyes connected in a strange and awkward new way that made me blush.

"See! I told you! You're totally freaked out. You should see how red your face is right now. Ha! You're totally embarrassed that I scared you."

That was a ploy because Aaron was pretty observant. He knew within a second that when I looked at him; I was into him. There's no way he didn't notice. This made me uncomfortable.

"Are you wearing perfume?" he asked.

"Oh. Yeah—no. I mean, Mom gave me a hug, so it's probably hers." Then I quickly segued to, "So I didn't know you had horses? Do you ride?"

"Na. My younger sister Janet does. Dad's the horse expert, but she took to it and now her and Dad train them and then go to these competitions in Pennsylvania. Boring shit, you know."

I nodded as if to agree with him. Then he got right to it.

"Do you have a girlfriend?" he asked.

"No."

"Boyfriend?" as he nudged me again and laughed as to ensure I knew he was joking.

"Neither."

"Wait? Does that mean you like both?"

I hesitated. How does one answer such an awkward question?

"No. Geez. I'm just not dating, you know?"

"That's cool. Me neither."

I stood up and walked over to the record player, moved the needle over to the 4th track, and said, "Now, this one; this one is my favorite song! I love this song. It's amazing."

Aaron laughed just a little and said, "What, 'Waiting for a Girl Like You'? Wow, that's kind of a chick song, but sure, whatever."

I silently took that as a compliment as the song played. I walked back over to his bed and sat down next to him, but this time I nudged him with my shoulder. But my nudge was noticeably a flirtatious nudge.

"Hey! You're not allowed to do that," he said with a laugh as he unexpectedly grabbed me and moved into the dominant position to wrestle. It didn't take long for him to pin me underneath him on the floor. He was a medalist on the school's wrestling team, and he knew all the right moves.

I looked up at him and said, "Okay, you got me. I give up."

At the same moment, he pinned me beneath him, the chorus of the song was playing, "I've been waiting for a girl like you to come into my life . . . " just as Aaron's younger sister Janet was walking by his room. Looking through the open door, she saw us locked in an intimately close and awkward embrace to a very popular love song. "Aww, just look at the lovebirds on the floor," she said sarcastically. "You two are so gay. Oh, my God. So, so gay."

Aaron, totally taken by surprise, quickly stood up. "Not a chance, idiot!" Then he slammed the door shut.

Now irreparably embarrassed and just standing confused in the middle of his room, I said. "I should go. It's almost dinnertime, anyway."

"She's an idiot. Don't let her get under your skin. Gay my ass," as he just let it all bounce off of him.

"What are you doing tomorrow?"

"Nothing."

"Wow! You sure do a lot of nothing. Come back over and let's hang out again."

"Sure. Yeah. Okay." I stumbled nervously all over my reply.

The next day, Saturday, I made my way across town again to Aaron's just after lunch. Aaron answered the door. "Everyone's out for the day. This place is totally mine until five o'clock. Let's blast some music."

Prelude to a Kiss

After walking up the stairs, he walked into the room first and abruptly stopped so I would bump into him.

"Hey! Are you trying to start something?" as he grabbed and threw me on his bed.

"Wow. Your Mom sure hugs you a lot. I smell the perfume again." Then, he asked me something I wasn't prepared to answer. "You have a thing for me, don't you?"

Nervously and instantly, I answered, "Don't be silly. What would make you think that?"

"I just thought maybe, after that look you gave me yesterday, that you well . . . "

"Well, what?" I softly demanded.

"You know," he said rather carefully.

"I'm not gay," I stated.

He moved in closer and replied, "Neither am I."

"I'm not sure I understand what you're trying to say."

He had just taken me completely off guard and my breathing became very labored with excitement and terror at the same time. Was he messing with me? Was he going to beat me up if I gave the wrong answer? Either way, I had to say something, fast.

I took a deep breath and for the very first time in my life, I divulged a tiny piece of my lifelong secret. "You don't understand. I'm really kind of different."

"Different?" he asked with a confused look.

"Yeah. It's way too weird to tell you though," as I stood up wildly uncomfortable with where this conversation was going.

"Tell me. I won't say anything. I promise."

It seemed as if time had stopped right at that moment. I didn't know how I would describe this to him in a way he'd understand.

"Well? I can't believe I'm about to tell you this. Swear on your life you won't tell anyone."

"Okay. Sure."

"No! Swear on your life!" I demanded.

"Okay. Okay. I swear. Wow, this must be a doozy," he answered.

What had I just gotten myself into? I have just committed to telling him about my lifelong secret. There was no going back from here. I also knew that whatever electricity I was feeling would dissipate by the time I finished divulging my secret. Regardless, I took a deep breath and forged ahead.

"Okay so, um. You're a guy, right?"

"Wow! Now that's a brilliant observation," he said sarcastically.

"Just stay quiet while I get this out. This is really, really hard." I continued with the cadence of an auctioneer. "So, when you see me, you see a guy. But something wrong must have happened when I came out of my Mom. I should have been born a girl, but somehow, here I am like this."

I looked away to prepare for an onslaught of hurtful jokes.

"Woah! Wait. What?" He started. "Hold on. Are you one of those trannies?"

His response was exactly what I feared. "No! This was a mistake. Forget it. I need to go," and I rushed out of his room, down the stairs, and out the side door of his house as I began to cry.

As I was making my way off his property, he chased me down and said, "Hey. Don't be so upset. It's okay. I'm not going to tell anyone. But you have to admit that's a little weird to hear, you know?" Then he continued, "A lot of us at school don't get you. You have been hard to figure out because one day you're hanging with the music geeks and other days with us. And honestly, some of us kind of thought you might be gay."

> So you're like one of those people trapped in the wrong body, right? Like on Donohue?

"I'm not gay."

"No. No. I'm not calling you gay. I'm just saying that hearing what you just said is crazy, like I didn't see it coming. Don't go home," he pleaded.

"Just don't make fun of me okay. You have no idea how hard it is to be like me," I said, wiping away my last tear.

Within a moment, he had me turned around, and we walked back to his house and into his room.

I crept to the bed and sat beside him, which, incidentally, was the only place to sit in his room other than the floor.

"Seriously, I won't say anything. I swear. So you're like one of those people trapped in the wrong body, right? Like on Donohue? Wow. That's got to be weird."

"You know about Donohue?" I asked with excitement.

"Yeah. I saw some tall English chick that used to be a dude but got an operation."

"Oh, my God. I saw that too. Yes. That's like me! But you need to know something. It's not fun. It's actually awful. And, I knew something was wrong by the time I was four."

"Holy shit! How did you know that young?"

"I don't know. I just did."

He moved in closer to me and looked directly into my eyes, which made me crazy and uncomfortable and said, "Is that why you like me?"

"Like you? Like, *like you*, like you? No."

"Are you sure?" He continued.

"You are acting weird."

Then in one quick motion, he moved in and kissed me. I thought, "How is this happening?" I kissed him back, and that was my first encounter with the butterflies. I had heard of it, but never understood what they were until this moment. If we were playing the game "seven minutes in heaven," then we just raised the bar for sure.

It was unbelievable. I was kissing one of the cutest, most popular guys in school. I was free falling into unfamiliar yet exhilarating territory. That day, Aaron made me feel like the girl I always knew I was. For the very first time in my life, I was actually *feeling*.

After our unruly session, I looked at him again and said, "Okay, so you understand this isn't gay, right? I mean, I know externally I'm a boy, but that isn't me."

"I understand. We can keep this our secret, okay? We have four hours before anyone comes home. Can we try something?" He asked.

"That depends I think."

Within seconds we were kissing again, but this time he was becoming much more aggressive. I knew he wasn't a virgin, and also knew where he was headed, so I gently pulled the plug, and said, "Maybe it's better we don't go there right now."

Although we kept kissing, he respected what I said. My racing heart, the amazing swarms of butterflies in my stomach, and a newfound desire that completely consumed me changed my outlook. It was overwhelming and yet, amazing. From that day on, I always wanted to be around him. I loved the way I felt whenever he was around. Yes! Those were feelings I wanted to have all the time. After two months, there was little doubt, I was falling in love with him. My first love, and that's when my virginity succumbed to the situation.

Soon, Aaron and I were finding our alone time anytime we could in his room. If someone was home, he'd shut and lock the door. Other times when we were alone, we would stay in his room for hours. I had sleepovers at his house on the weekends until summer came and we were having two to three sleepovers a week.

During one particular sleepover, Aaron forgot to shut his bedroom door as we fooled around. During a moment of what was becoming very intimate, Aaron's sister Janet walked by the door. Both of us, like deer caught in the headlights, knew that if she saw us, she would have said something. Instead of worrying, Aaron slowly and quietly shut his door so we could continue.

While lying in bed, looking up at his ceiling, he asked, "What was your first orgasm? Where were you and how did you do it?"

"Really? God! Why are you asking me that? That's embarrassing and the way it happened is nothing you'd understand, anyway. Trust me."

"Oh, come on," he insisted as he handed me a piece of Big Red cinnamon gum.

"God. Why do you need to know this?" I growled back. "Okay. But don't laugh." I paused briefly to grab some invisible courage so I could tell him some intimate details. "I would tuck *the thing* between my legs, so I could see my flat front in the full-length mirror. Then I would go over to my bed, and um . . . " I paused again.

"And what?" Aaron asked.

"Well, I would rub my body, specifically my pelvic region up and down against the side of the bed over and over. There was this one time that within less than a minute, I had the most amazing feeling."

Psychologically the feeling and how I produced it was profound. I equated this new mysterious feeling to God finally granting me my lifelong wish; making my body correct.

"Wow, you are so odd. That sounds like what a girl would do. What I mean is, wow, that's definitely not the way dudes experience their first orgasm."

Our very private relationship would last for just over seven months. At school, we ensured our secret relationship stayed secret. It was as if we barely knew each other. But at home, it was different; wonderful. Sadly, I knew this wasn't going to last because Aaron was always flirting with all the girls in school every day. But I just stayed in the moment and refused to think about the future. I loved him. Although I never spoke it aloud, I could hear myself say, "Aaron. I love you."

"Hey. Do you want to go over to Randy's house tonight?" he asked.

This took me by surprise because I had never really been invited to an outing like this before. Secretly, I also found Randy to be dangerously attractive. He was that tough, independent guy that no one messed with, but all the guys secretly envied his bold confidence. Just being near him was alluring to me. But more so, I wanted to be near his sister. Randy had an enormous family, but one sister always stood out to me—Lisa. She was four years older than me and I noticed her from day one of junior high. She was so beautiful, very popular, and someone I desperately wanted or wished I could emulate. Actually, every member of Lisa's family was beautiful.

When we arrived at Randy's house we sat in the dining room and within a few minutes his sister Lisa entered the adjacent room. There she was. I could not take my eyes off of her. She completely mesmerized me. My attraction to her was not the same attraction I held for Aaron or Randy. It was an attraction more akin to longing. I aspired to be like her like so many other girls did. The way she dressed, the way she did her hair, the way she carried herself. She possessed every quality I so desperately wanted for myself. I wanted to be just like Lisa.

> She possessed every quality I so desperately wanted for myself.

Randy motioned for us to go upstairs to his room. I wanted to stay behind so I could meet Lisa and talk to her, even for just a few minutes. I made my way upstairs with the group, to his room where they played some Black Sabbath records. I didn't know, nor did I understand this kind of music. To me, it was terrible! But I sat there on his bed, giving it my best team effort.

That was when Randy opened his window and lit a joint. I had never even seen marijuana before, let alone been invited to partake. One by one they would take a hit and pass it to the next person. Then another guy, Keith, tried to pass it to me.

"No, it's okay I really don't want to do this."

"Just take it. Don't be a puss."

"No. I really don't want to do this. I'm sorry." I repeated with more conviction.

"Wow, what a chick." He laughed.

Randy, releasing a waft of smoke from his mouth and out the opened window, turned around and walked over towards me. I was getting very nervous. He put his hand on my shoulder and said, "You know something Eddie, I like you. I like the way you stand up for yourself. You don't have to do this if you don't want to and I think that's cool. Keith. Shut the fuck up dickhead and leave Eddie alone. He's cool with me." He said matter-of-factly, but in some guy-club humorous way, I didn't quite understand.

He stood me up and gave me one of those guy hugs. You know, the hug two guys give each other just after combat? But to me, it was a hug from a hot teenage guy. From that day forward, this person I was afraid of in school became my friend. Someone I was happy to know. Even after high school, we would see each other around town. He had a respect for me and I for him.

Things seemed to be going rather well with Aaron. We were still enjoying each other's company, and I felt more and more confident with each passing day. Until . . .

∽

They say you never forget your first love. God knows I never did. But that was not necessarily a wonderful thing for me. It was just before Halloween during lunch, when in the lunch line I saw Aaron standing about four students ahead of me. He was talking to a few of his friends. At one point, they laughed, as if a joke was told, except I noticed Aaron was not laughing with them.

At that same moment, Aaron turned around and looked directly at me. As always, his look made my heart flutter. But this time he had an unfamiliar look in his eyes. I didn't like this look. It looked almost as if he was enraged. He quickly approached me, and without a millisecond of notice, punched me in the solar plexus and then once across the jaw, sending me flying out of the lunch line and onto the cafeteria floor.

At that very moment, the lunchroom noise fell to a whisper, and all eyes were on me. Almost immediately, tears welled up within me and began to release in a soft, almost unnoticeable way. More than a hundred classmates were staring at me and all I could think was, "What kind of craziness is this? Why would Aaron do this to me? What did I do to deserve this?"

I assumed someone must have somehow found out about us, and Aaron thought it was my fault.

"No," I thought. "I never told anyone about our relationship." Feeling helpless, embarrassed, violated, and discarded, I knew I could have picked myself up, faced everyone in the lunchroom, and outed Aaron to the entire student body. But that would also *out me*, and I was just not capable of dealing with that kind of humiliation and awkwardness. And besides, that style of vengeful viciousness was not a part of my persona.

The boys in the lunch line were laughing as the girls told them to stop being such idiots. Then, the principal of the school, who had witnessed the entire incident within an instant, came up behind Aaron. He grabbed him by his ear, twisting it with excruciating fervor, and dragged him off to the office. A teacher helped me up from the floor and walked me to the nurse's office.

Upon arriving at the nurse's office, and after explaining why I was there, I told the nurse, "I'm okay. I'm fine. Can I just go to my next class?"

I was lying, of course. My jaw was throbbing, and I was still barely breathing from the blow to my midsection. And to top it off, my emotions were completely and utterly wrecked. The punch to the face left only a small blemish, which could easily be explained away as a gym class mishap. I could have none of this revealed to Mom and Dad. The fear of my family learning of the relationship that I had with Aaron wasn't something I was prepared to deal with.

From that day forward, Aaron and I ceased to exist. He gave no explanations and no apologies. In fact, he never said another word to me. I had no closure. The relationship we enjoyed for so many months completely vaporized in just a matter of minutes. I was fourteen years old and completely broken. Not only did I see myself as a circus freak, but apparently I was not worthy of love either.

Everything that I knew since I was four years old was so much more intense—so much rawer. And it was this rawness that led me into one of the darkest times of my life.

6

Fatally Wrecked

Aaron wrecked me. I became disconnected from everything and everyone, with no one the wiser. All that remained were the unpleasant things life had presented me. In fact, one of the few thoughts that remained was, "A person like me can't be loved. It's far too dangerous."

In the weeks that followed, I became more and more reclusive, relegating myself to my bedroom. My typical excuse for this reclusiveness was my need to be creative; to write music or teach myself how to program a computer. I was a seasoned professional at masking my truth, numbing my emotions, and hiding my true identity to just about everyone. And everyone now included Mom.

Music was always my go-to; something I suppose I was predestined to do. I could pen my emotions in poetic form, add my own beautiful melodies, and record them in my tiny makeshift bedroom studio. The melancholy melodies seemed to flow effortlessly from my fingers to specific notes and chords on my piano keyboard, as if I had possessed the piano itself. As I hummed melodies, I soon found myself writing the words that formed out of the melodic hums and within only a couple of weeks, those words became the lyrics to over twenty-five love songs. Hearing my emotions being transformed into something bigger than myself gave me a brief rush and a genuine sense of accomplishment.

I also gravitated toward computers. I found that with a computer, I could transport myself to a world of my own creation. I had taught myself languages unknown to most other students my age. Computer programming languages that could help me create just about anything my imagination could conjure up. My thought was that maybe it could help shape my world into something that I could control.

Darkness dominated the fall months in upstate New York, as each day grew shorter. The melodies on my piano also grew darker, as did my ability to stay preoccupied with the little universe of zeros and ones I had been creating on my computer.

> All the colors surrounding me suddenly faded into several darkened shades of gray. Everything literally went colorless in an instant.

My incongruity, along with continuous bouts with name-calling and bullying, and most prominently Aaron, had taken my broken heart and set it on a collision course with utter despondency. I wept. I was so angry at God for birthing me into such an impossible life.

"Why couldn't you just fix me?" I shouted.

The extreme internal pain of always being incongruent gave way to new, terrifying thoughts of a meaningless future. A future where I not only felt relentless pain but a future where I was hurting or disappointing everyone else that loved me.

I found myself journaling again. "I don't belong here!" I wrote just beyond the pool of tears blurring everything. "I don't know how to do this anymore!" I continued. "I love everyone so much, but no one will ever understand *me*. They'll all end up hating me while locking me away in some juvenile institution, thinking I'm crazy."

I paused and looked around my bedroom as everything changed in an instant. All the colors surrounding me suddenly faded into several darkened shades of gray. Everything literally went colorless in an instant. In what would be the most vulnerable moment of my life, I made my way to the bathroom medicine cabinet, chocked full of prescription pills.

I grabbed every bottle. I didn't even know what I grabbed or if what I grabbed would help me fade into oblivion or not, but I was now willing to find out.

But again, my love for Mom, Dad, and Colleen crept back in. This gave me great pause, as I reflected on the effect this would have on the family. I wept stronger as I slowly dumped the various pills into separate piles on the bed.

"Can I really do this? God! Please give me something! I'm begging you! Please answer me at least once! Out of all the days I've been asking you to help me, help me now!" I paused as if to hear the voice of God speak. But all fell quiet.

"Goddammit! Please!" I cried out.

The only thing left to do was to confront every exposed part of my beautiful, lost soul; to allow myself to let go. To swallow every pill laid out before me.

"Should I talk to Mom once more and let her in on my depression? Should I tell her that my lifelong struggle is far bigger than she thinks?"

Although lethally depressed, I still felt conflicted as I reached for the first pill. Then—a quiet knock came as my bedroom door opened. In a panic, I covered the pills under the blankets.

It was Dad. Hiding my face from him so I would not reveal my fatal brokenness, I crackled out, "Hi."

"I need you to bring more firewood in from the garage. It's going to be freezing tonight. Just throw a few loads into the basement for the woodstove. I'll be out to help you in a few minutes."

He left; blissfully unaware of the finality that he just interrupted. With my heart racing, I put all the pills back into their respective bottles and placed them back exactly where I had found them. I put on my winter outerwear and trekked outside to do exactly as Dad had instructed.

Not fully known to me, I realized that I had just experienced a very spiritual moment. The invisible hand of God led my dad directly to my room at exactly the right time. Dad just saved my life and he had no idea.

How to Successfully Fail at Assimilation

Keeping myself busy seemed the only way to stay out of the darkness I was experiencing every day. I went from despondent and suicidal to burning the candle at both ends within days. Looking back, I honestly don't know how I survived. For the first few years, I spent much of my time in self-isolation whenever I was home. My schedule was simple yet busy, which kept me from focusing on my incongruity. I'd go to school, come home, do homework, write music, write more music, then teach myself computer programming. When I got around to it, I would sleep a little, then repeat the same schedule the next day. And it seemed to work. I was so preoccupied with so many aspects of creativity within myself that I could, at least for part of the day, keep my incongruity at bay.

There was no way I would ever put myself in a position of being bullied, teased, or assaulted ever again. "I'm a boy and I like girls," I repeated to myself over and over. I wanted this phrase to brainwash me. The only question I had after repeating the phrase a thousand times was, "How do I stop liking guys? And how do I tell my brain to stop telling me I'm a girl?"

Instead of focusing on brainwashing myself, I continued to dive deeper into my music. I also focused on attempting to date. By the

Hiding From Myself

> *Intimacy felt so unnatural with a woman, I would always end up in my head.*

age of eighteen, I immersed myself in not-so-casual relationships with several women. I lost my virginity again, to an older woman. Lost my virginity again? Yes. I had two unique experiences based on if they were male or female. Aaron always gave me butterflies and sent my heart swirling. But the women I engaged with did nothing remotely close. Maybe I needed more practice? Maybe I was hindering myself; subconsciously blocking myself from experiencing authentic emotions with these women?

To the dismay of many people that knew me, intimacy felt so unnatural with a woman, I would always end up in my head. I had to play a secret game of role reversal where I would become them and they would become me.

There was one time each year that I could get a break, a free pass to be a little more me. Halloween. My sister was the first to get out of the car after driving nearly an hour to get to the dance club in New Paltz, NY. Second was one of my best friends, Shannon. She was one of the first kids I had ever met. She was also my first kiss at five years old. The sneaky little promiscuous shits we were. Whenever she and my sister were together, we were sure to have a blast. I was last to get out of the car, wearing my predictable costume, a rather conservatively dressed woman. This wasn't a costume or gag to me.

We went up to the sales window outside of the club to pay the $20 cover charge. A sign read, "LADIES. NO COVER." As I was handing the girl the money she pointed to the sign and said, "Where's your costume girl?" Then she waved all of us in! This was definitely a wonderful start to the evening, a real confidence builder. The entire night in the darkly lit nightclub, I secretly hoped a cute guy would offer to buy me a drink. A girl can dream, right?

~

Her name was Karen. My latest attempt at a relationship and one that would forever change me in ways I couldn't possibly comprehend.

Karen represented a new attraction for me. She was pretty and a lot of fun. I thought she had the most contagious smile. What was even more attractive about Karen, was her sense of humor and her unmistakable laugh. We started dating while I was in a local cover band that gigged all around the New York Tri-state area. She became my biggest fan at gigs. To say she was devoted to me would be an understatement.

Even though I believed that I fell in love with her, I was still conflicted. "Do I *really* love Karen romantically?" I'd ask myself relentlessly. "Yeah. I must. Right?" I reassured the invisible therapist in my head.

However, what I couldn't come to terms with was the unavoidable truth that I wanted to *be* her, not necessarily *with* her.

"Jesus Christ, I'm a complete mess!" I admitted to the still present therapist.

It seemed I was creating more questions than answers with my little self-moderated therapy sessions. I figured out that part of the reason I had been doing so well with this relationship was that other aspects of my day were so booked, that I had very little time for my "self" to be annoying me. I landed a full-time job at a college I had previously attended. I was in a successful band. I was an aspiring songwriter. And I was running my own business. I was definitely burning the candle at both ends. And it was helping to quell the unpleasantness of my dysphoria and my natural attraction to men.

I was swimming in a sea of confusion and dissonance. There I was, playing house with a wonderful woman who loved me, yet every time I'd see a cute guy my heart would palpitate. Every time we made love, I was in my head again. Deep down in that place I had bricked off to the rest of the world was a woman that desperately needed her freedom and desired to be loved by a man. I could feel her within me busily dismantling that brick wall I had spent so long building—slowly, brick by brick.

For the rest of our doomed relationship, I never gained the courage to out myself to her. Instead, I ended things terribly and without closure. I completely screwed her over. I hated myself for what I had done. But instead of dealing with my truth and my faults, I moved on with someone else, who would later become my first wife.

By the age of twenty-three, I was engaged to Melana. She was astonishingly beautiful and one of my shortest relationships. The marriage lasted about a year, which included the birth of my first child; a son, Corey.

I was getting divorced and the idea of it scared me to death. I was being thrust into the single parent club. Although we ended up with joint custody of Corey, disturbingly I was hearing more and more horror stories from him. This forced my hand which brought us back into the courtroom.

"I won't ever let anything or anyone ever hurt you again," I assured him. He would cry and hug me so tightly as he whimpered, "I love you Daddy," as his tiny face and tears made contact with my cheek. I spent every bit of my savings attempting to protect Corey. Over $40,000 evaporated within a multi-year bitter divorce and custody case; a case that lasted far longer than the marriage itself. I had been saving that money for years. It was my transition money to have *The Surgery*. I was dealt a shitty hand that had put me *all-in* with a more important priority—protecting my baby boy.

With the divorce finally behind me, and already in another serious relationship, I began focusing on my music again. Writing and producing music seemed to be the one thing in my life that could carry me through any storm. The person I was dating, Christine, who would later become my second wife, always appeared genuinely interested in my music.

She was in several performances in high school; one of them was truly inspiring. It was the day of her big performance in the high school play *Bye Bye Birdie*. While readying herself for her performance, she saw that the kerosene heater within her house was running hot. She walked over to turn it down and before she knew what happened, it blew up in her face. Within moments the ensuing fire engulfed her entire house in flames with her precious dog trapped inside. Despite this tragic event, she had gone on with her high school play that evening. She was the epitome of "The show must go on." Her perseverance and determination moved me incredibly. This inspired me to do something very special.

I met Margaret one summer while working at a small community college near my hometown. She was in the area for only part of the summer, but we found each other easy to relate to and quickly became friends; talking for hours on end some days. She was an aspiring actress who not only wanted to be on Broadway but was determined to make it happen. By the time I had met Christine, Margaret had already landed the role of a lifetime on Broadway in the smash hit, *Miss Saigon*.

As the cast took their final bows to a continuous standing ovation, we made our way out of the theatre.

"Wow, that was amazing!" Christine said emotionally.

As we exited back onto the sidewalk along Broadway, I began walking towards the side of the theatre.

"Where are you going? Don't we have to go this way?" she asked, pointing up Broadway.

"I know where I'm going, Chrissy. Come on now," I said playfully.

She watched in what appeared to be sheer horror, as I made my way up the five stairs to the backstage entryway and knocked on the door.

"Oh my God! What are you doing?" she said more forcefully. "You're gonna get us in trouble."

The door opened, and a guy looked at me and said, "Can I help you?"

"I'm Eddie. We're here to . . . "

He cut in smiling and shouted, "Eddie! We're all expecting you two. Come on in. I'm Jason." He continued to hold the door open for Christine. "And you must be Christine, right?"

Christine's moment of horror had just transformed into dizzying confusion as she made her way inside to catch up with me, while quietly saying, "Hi. Yes."

"What is happening right now? How did you do this? Oh my God, I'm going to cry," she said all at once as a tear of happy surprise formed.

"I'll give you a tour of our stage first if you don't mind." Jason then focused his attention on Christine. After all, this experience was for her. We walked out onto the empty raked stage. For clarification, a raked stage is a stage that creates added depth perception to the audience as it slopes upwards and away from the front of the stage. The slope created is the rake, and *Miss Saigon* had the steepest rake in the industry.

I will never forget the wonder in her eyes as she stood center stage, where just moments before, the entire cast performed in front of a sold-out audience. She stood silently looking up into the layers of balconies and seats, taking it all in. After giving her the backstage grand tour, including the complex multi-floor prop elevators under the stage, Jason led us to the dressing room to meet up with Margaret and the cast.

"Eddie!" Margaret raised her arms to give me a hug. "I'm so happy you are here!" She then introduced herself. "And you must be Christine. It's so nice to meet you. When Eddie called to set this up, I was so happy to hear about the big surprise in store for you. I invited you both to our after performance get-together, but unfortunately, we are all miserably sick. But you know, the show must go on," she explained as several other cast members joined in affirming her. "And we heard about your heartbreaking, yet inspiring story from your performance in high school the day you lost your house and dog to a fire. That's incredible!"

Several years later Christine and I married, and from a distance, it seemed everything was going wonderfully. We just bought a beautiful house in the Catskill Mountains and right on a cul-de-sac. Between my job, my successful side business, and my music, it would seem everything was on track. I was getting more voice-over work, radio spots, and live concert introductions. I had also just finished building a recording studio, and we were about to have our first child together.

But through it all Christine and I became rather distant to each other. Much of the distance was my fault because everything was still just so unnatural. I kept asking myself, "What have I done? I just married another woman, and once again prevented any possibility of transitioning."

It was during these times I had already been secretly self-administering hormones to myself. Christine discovered I had been going through her closet, which would aggravate her. Although she knew about me, I don't think she truly understood how real my conundrum was. Although I had gone through her closet several times, I didn't fancy dressing in her clothing because to me I looked dreadful. I also didn't care for her fashion sense, to be honest (although several years later I would come to appreciate it). To me, I looked the exact opposite of the way I should. What Christine didn't know is that for the better part of my life I had tremendous difficulty looking in a mirror. While she understood that I had gender dysphoria, I don't think she realized just how far that rabbit hole went.

After our son Matthew was born, we found out she was pregnant again. She would have our second child, and my third son, Tyler three days short of a year from the birth of Matthew.

Hiding From Myself

While she was pregnant with Tyler, I became a producer for a regional offshoot of *American Idol*. Some cast members from the HBO hit series, *The Sopranos*, and the movie *Goodfellas* organized the competition. Almost immediately I received a call asking if I might want to co-produce the show. I did not want to pass up that opportunity, so I said yes—and within two weeks I was not just co-producing the show, I was actually the producer of the show. That little production in a Catskill hotel was the starting point of the most active part of my music career. I spent all of my time working on the show. I wasn't giving Christine the attention she needed and deserved. I was doing what I knew how to do, and I was avoiding what I didn't know how to do.

It was during that show that I found out something that would alter and eventually end the marriage. I responded to the situation poorly. I would use what I had found out as an excuse to start an inappropriate relationship, with one of the winners of the show I was producing.

Several years later that person would become my third wife. We were traveling back and forth to Nashville many times a year. I was writing and producing more music than I had done in a long time while building a name. I wrote and produced a lot of songs within that time, including a crossover-country track that topped an independent chart in the UK. That track would open some doors that would lead us to work with some of the best songwriters and notable artists in Nashville.

The one thing that was still always present was my incongruity. But rather than face it, I eventually ended up moving to Florida. The decision to move was incredibly complex. The struggle I had dealt with for decades had always told me I would need to move away from small town USA to land myself on a better trajectory towards successfully transitioning. More importantly, I was making a decision that would affect my boys, Matthew, Tyler, and Corey. I made them two promises. The first was that I would call or Skype them every single day. The second was that I would be on a flight every four to six weeks to spend four days with them, and we would also have six consecutive weeks in the summer and just under two weeks during Christmas and New Year's break together in Florida. I kept my promises, and we made it work.

The reality is I am a dad and a woman, and proud of it.

> The reality is I am a dad and a woman, and proud of it.

As hard as the decision to move was (and it was harder than I could have ever suspected), I knew it was what I had to do. But I began feeling more and more isolated. This feeling had its roots in my three boys. My quick decision had placed me in a position where I could no longer hop in the car and forty-five minutes later watch them in a school sports game or weekend league. I could no longer do the same for school functions such as plays and concerts. It weighed on me heavier than anything else ever had, even my incongruity.

Over the next few years, the change never became easier. In fact, it became much harder. It proved so difficult that I found myself in the same situation again, and about to have my fourth son, Jack. No matter the outside perception of the situation with all the devastation and destruction, all of my children represent beauty in my life. It's amazing how children can change your life so positively and profoundly. The love that I have for each of my boys is so incredible that the English language isn't worthy to describe it. Just about every loving parent would say the same thing.

I am the dad of four wonderful boys. I will always be their dad. That title doesn't magically change because I am now facing and living my authenticity. Do I wish I was a mom? Of course I do. But the reality is I am a dad *and* a woman, and proud of it.

A Close Encounter of the Me Kind

Working per diem for a trade show registration company had its perks. I was flying to just about every major city in the United States, working at various trade shows and business conferences and meeting tens of thousands of people from all over the world. The workday was always long and tiring, but after hours it was a different story. Kirk, the owner of the company, spared no expense having us experience the best of the best restaurants and things to do around the country. I had seen some dinner and drinking tabs for just the two of us that were in the four-digit range.

It was also during these trips, typically between five to ten days in duration, I would find people like myself, but already living authentically. The city didn't matter, because they all had their own slice of the demographic to which I belonged.

My first gig was in New Orleans, just after Mardi Gras. I was 21 and excited to go because I knew there would be a large transgender community there. I thought about how I could get some alone time to go explore.

It was early in the afternoon when Kirk and I arrived in town. It didn't take long to decide that we'd start by going straight to Bourbon Street right after checking into the Hilton Riverwalk Hotel, a beautiful hotel situated right on the big bend of the Mississippi. It was about a ten-minute walk to the French Quarter, and within no time at all, we had arrived. It was only three o'clock in the afternoon and there were already hundreds of people beginning to flood the streets. It seemed to be a perpetual, never-ending party.

We stopped at a street-side window and ordered two tall Hurricanes.

"Drink it really slow," Kirk warned. "This stuff will knock you down faster than its name."

"Wow. Okay," I said, as I took my first sip through the large straw. "They apparently made my Hurricane a weak sun shower, Kirk. Mine tastes like Kool-Aid."

"That's what I'm trying to warn you about. You won't even see it coming. Trust me. Drink it slowly."

We walked up and down Bourbon Street for a few hours, stopping every so often to sit and listen to one of the countless jazz, zydeco, and rock bands that occupied just about every venue along the strip. Besides the drinks, the atmosphere and the energy was intoxicating. After ordering some local Creole food for dinner, we continued down the street. It was near impossible to walk in a straight line, not because we were already intoxicated, but because there were now thousands of people everywhere.

It was the strangest mixture of smells I had ever experienced. A strange and pungent stench of alcohol and urine, mixed with the delicious smell of andouille sausage and jambalaya, left me confused, and quite possibly, emotionally scarred for life. But what made things wildly more complex was the scent each of the thousands of people made while clashing with one another—too much Ralph Lauren here, a little too much Tommy Girl there. At that point I didn't know whether I was fortunate to have my senses dampened by the Hurricanes or if it was just going to make me sick altogether.

Midnight came fast. We found ourselves towards one end of Bourbon Street and made our way into a quiet bar and strip club.

We breezed through the front entrance, which to the right side, displayed a huge Marquis of the performers. We made our way to a table inside the dimly lit and still fairly busy club and waited for our waitress. Almost immediately upon sitting down, our waitress, who was topless, came over to take our order. Kirk spoke for the two of us and said we'll have two drafts.

She thanked us and went on to get our drinks. She was stunning. There was something about her that intrigued me. I couldn't put my finger on it, but there was something about her that subconsciously called out to me. Kirk typically stayed quiet with such things because he was a very faithful man to his beautiful wife. In fact, I was wondering just how drunk he had to be for us to even be in this club.

Then it happened. Kirk whispered over to me. "I want you to turn around. Do it slowly, then look behind the bar at the platform that goes up to the ceiling and tell me what you see."

I casually turned around and looked behind the bar. I saw the platform at about a thirty-degree angle that made its way up to the ceiling. Laying down on this platform was a nude individual; like head to toe naked. Upon that first look, I noticed just how gorgeous she was.

"Yeah, she's beautiful and looks like a model," I said, as I looked back toward Kirk.

"No. Look closer," he commanded.

Once again I turned around and looked. Okay, she had a penis. This didn't bother me, but now I understood why Kirk was saying what he was saying. This was far too uncomfortable for him. So I turned back to him and said, "Yes I see. She's a transsexual. Is that a problem?"

He then noticed all the other girls in the room. And with a complete look of shock and bewilderment, he looked back at me and said, "We can't stay here. Everybody in this place is a tranny!"

He grabbed a $20 bill and put it on the table and told me it was time for us to go. Before I could convince him to stop worrying, he had already stood up to make his way out the door. The waitress who was already heading back to our table saw us leaving, so I put my arms up in the air to signal *I don't know* while pointing to the twenty on the table. I even mouthed the words, "I'm sorry."

As we stood in front of the club, Kirk saw the photos on the Marquee that showed each of the performers. He looked me straight in the eyes and he said, "Not a word of this to anyone—ever. Understand?"

I laughed, and said, "Fine, but I don't understand why we had to leave? I don't know what you found so uncomfortable?"

We spent the next half hour walking back to the hotel.

Right before he opened the door to his room, he said, "I'll meet you at seven tomorrow morning. Have a good night." Then I walked a few doors down the hallway to my room. I went into my room, but only to see how I looked and to fix myself. I knew I had to go back to that bar. So I went back out and made a beeline straight to that club on the opposite side of Bourbon Street in the gay district.

As I re-entered the club, the same waitress was still there and said, "Hey honey. Where's your friend?"

"He was pretty tired and wanted to leave. And, well, I wanted to come back as soon as I could."

She said, "That sounds like a plan. What can I get you? It's on me."

"Can I get a Cosmo?"

"Look at you, Mijo. Absolutely."

I sat down at the same table we had left about an hour earlier and just looked around the room with lots of curiosity.

When she came back to the table, she looked at me and said, "My name is Jessica."

"Hi Jessica, my name is Eddie," I replied nervously. "Would you mind if I ask you a quick question?"

"Go right ahead, sugar. Ask away."

"Is everyone in here transsexual? And before you answer, the reason I'm asking is that I was born different and somehow I ended up looking like this. My reason for coming back is to meet you, hoping I can figure out how to navigate my struggle."

She was such a sweetheart. "Aww, Mija." Just a moment ago, she used Mijo, which I knew was the male form of the term, honey. She was now addressing me in the feminine.

"If you've got twenty minutes, stick around and a few of us will be over to talk to you. I take it you're not out yet?"

> They were so authentic, transparent, and unapologetic. They exuded a confidence to which I was not yet familiar.

"No. That's one of my problems and biggest fears always plaguing my life."

"Well, don't you worry. You've got some new friends right here that will be happy to talk to you."

It was nearly one-thirty in the morning, so I knew this would end up being a long night, but oh so worth it.

I sat with the most beautiful women I had laid eyes upon. Their transformation was nothing less than remarkable. They ranged in age from twenty-two to forty-two. What I learned from each one of them, I carry with me to this moment. They were so authentic, transparent, and unapologetic. They exuded a confidence to which I was not yet familiar.

I never would see any of them again. However, I left that club that early morning with a sense of undeniable freedom and determination to start my own transition as soon as possible. I just needed to build up an almost insurmountable amount of confidence so I too could begin HRT.

Hormones—From Mess to Miracle

Disclaimer: In this chapter, I discuss the practice of self-medication/administration of hormones for MTF individuals. Please note, I highly discourage this practice as it can be dangerous, even deadly. Do NOT self-medicate. Instead, put on your big girl pants and go see your doctor, so they can provide the proper blood tests and monitor you every step of the way. If I learned anything to impart to the reader considering this practice, my advice would be, "Fuck embarrassment. You're wasting valuable time holding onto your irrational fear and putting yourself at significant risk while doing so."

I rushed to the post office to check my newly opened secret P.O. box. In eager anticipation, I unlocked my box and there it was. A small box containing breast growth cream and some herbal supplements that, when used together, promised body feminization, in particular to help develop your breasts. Something inside of me knew it had to be too good to be true. My gut was already telling me all I was doing was feeding a snake oil industry that profited on the desperation of people like myself. But it was all I thought was available to me. I was twenty-two, desperate, and gullible.

After a couple months of reorders, I finally shook myself into reason and stopped. Nothing had changed. I would have expected the copious amounts of cream I had been applying would have at least made my skin softer. But no—nothing.

I began researching herbal supplements. Over the next several years I would purchase and attempt to come up with every possible concoction of various phytoestrogens; plant-based estrogens, herbs, and foods that I hoped would work. I began drinking expensive soy milk and spearmint tea, sprinkling flaxseed on my food, and taking the herb black cohosh. Still nothing.

It wasn't long after, feeling defeated, that while visiting my parents I found Mom's supply of unused hormone replacement therapy (HRT) pill packs. She was not very religious about taking her pills. In fact, she had amassed quite a few unopened pill packs. Knowing she wouldn't miss one of them, I took one of the unused packs and began taking one pill a day for the next twenty-eight days. Let's cut right to the chase. The pills did shit, nada, absolutely nothing. Nothing I had been trying was doing a darn thing.

I began to research how the endocrine system worked and how different hormones and specifically HRT affected the body. I went to libraries and read countless medical journals. Then I found it. A study monitoring the effects of HRT on transitioning individuals. It seemed the missing key wasn't in the introduction of estrogen; it was the removal, or lowering of my testosterone levels. Let's be honest, I was stuck inside the body of a horny, virile young man, which most likely meant my testosterone was as high as Mt. Everest. I learned that by not lowering testosterone levels; it prohibited the estrogen from doing its intended job. Second, Mom's HRT pill packs contained seven pills that were placebo pills. This way you keep a consistent routine by taking a pill every day to match your cycle. These pills

Hormones—From Mess to Miracle

were of such a low dose that even if my testosterone level was where it needed to be, there would be little if no change. And last, even if I was on a HRT plan tailored for me, it would take months and months before any noticeable changes would occur, anyway. All I had was a single pill pack and a dream. I was fighting a steep learning curve, doing things this way. I knew that someday I would have to find the courage to tell my doctor, or perhaps travel one hundred miles down the road to New York City to see another doctor that understood transgender issues.

But then the entire world changed. Right in the nick of time came—the Internet. Thank God for the Internet. I could finally search scores of enormous libraries, research university resources, and other sites all from a single search query. Suddenly research took on a whole new, exciting, and accessible meaning. Besides using the search engines available at the time—Yahoo, Alta-vista, Lycos, and a few others—I also began using several bulletin board services and primitive chat services. It didn't take long before I could connect to and communicate with other people just like me.

I met a trans woman online named Vickie. She lived in San Francisco and had told me she was nearly two-and-a-half years into transition. I told her what I had been doing and why I was still afraid to see a doctor.

"Honey, don't be wasting your money on that craziness. That stuff don't work," she explained. "You know, there're ways to get hormones without a prescription, right?"

I had finally found my pot of gold at the end of some overseas rainbow.

She piqued my interest. "Really? How?" I typed furiously.

"There's an overseas pharmacy that'll ship you up to three months of hormones without a prescription. I have a few DIY girlfriends that use them with no issues. But there're some drawbacks, okay? First. It's crazy expensive. Second. You need to make sure you order no more than three months at a time so your package doesn't get flagged by US Customs. Oh, and this is important, baby girl. It's dangerous as fuck! So be smart and don't rush it! Be careful, and start slow. Pay close attention to your entire body. Other than that, it's easy peasy."

"Okay, how do I start????"

She typed in a web address and a phone number. And just like that, I was on my way to placing my first order. In the rush of it all, I felt sneaky. I was being dishonest to my girlfriend, who at the time was living with me. I had finally found my pot of gold at the end of some overseas rainbow and made a decision that could forever change my life—and she had no idea.

I was so desperate that being deceptive didn't even cross my mind. I had purposely ignored one of the most fundamental traits that made me a good person: my honesty. The honesty that stays true along a winding road was now hiding behind a shroud of desperation.

I was playing directly into my insecurities. I dwelled on the prospect of being unloved and alone if she knew who I really was—if anyone knew. I was simultaneously perpetuating my complex tug-of-war with assimilation; of being that *guy* everyone thought I was. It was exhausting and never changed the fact that I knew each night while sleeping next to her: I was on the wrong side of the bed spooned up against a body I wished was mine.

I browsed their website, which by today's standards, would be considered utterly broken. But as primitive as it was, I found the exact items I needed. I wrote the item numbers and costs, then called in my order; a three-month supply of spironolactone and estradiol.

Spironolactone (spiro) is a drug typically used to treat congestive heart failure and high blood pressure, among other things. But it also has a fortunate side effect. It works to lower androgen levels in the body. In other words, it's amazing at lowering testosterone, which gives way to another fortunate side effect called gynecomastia, which is the enlargement of breast tissue. I was incredibly anxious as I awaited delivery. They said it would take between twelve and twenty days, mostly because of a slow Customs process.

On the twenty-second day, I made my daily run to the post office to check my medium-sized P.O. box. There it was—a large bulky envelope that had obviously been cut open by the U.S. Customs and resealed. My heart was jumping out of my chest with exhilaration. I grabbed it and raced back to my car with the package opened before I even opened the car door. I began with a low dose. This would allow me to see how my body responded, and if there were any reactions or side effects before bumping the dosage up. I knew that if I did not get my testosterone down first, I was wasting my time. This stuff cost me a small fortune and there was no way I was wasting any of it.

I took the spironolactone for the first three weeks before introducing the estrogen. Those first three weeks didn't have any noticeable effect on me, except for the undying need to pee all the time. Spironolactone is also a diuretic. I also read that I would need to stay more hydrated than normal. I knew this would be a very long ride. At the three-week mark, I added estradiol. And within a week of that, I introduced a second 2mg estradiol pill in the evening with my second dose of spironolactone.

Finally, I noticed and felt some subtle changes. My areolas seemed to be a little puffy, and my nipples ached. I was ecstatic! It was working! I began calling those pill bottles, "my miracle of womanhood in a bottle."

Within only two months, there was a notable difference in the shape of my chest. I had tiny breast buds forming under each of my nipples, which by now had increased by nearly a centimeter in diameter. I found it becoming more and more uncomfortable to take a shower without having pain from the water spraying down onto them. I recall accidentally bumping my chest into a door jamb which made me scream four-letter words loudly. I was thinking I was in need of a training bra or something to protect that area, not to mention they were poking out ever so slightly.

But the changes didn't stop there. There were other things I noticed. My skin seemed softer. My face was becoming much dryer and definitely needed daily maintenance and moisturizing. And I seemed to be slowly losing my sex drive. I just wasn't *in the mood* as often as I used to be.

The third month had arrived, and I was getting short on supplies. But there was actually a more pressing issue. I didn't have enough money to make another purchase. The last order was several hundred dollars, and I just didn't have it. When I took those last pills, it felt as if the dream was over. I knew that once I stopped taking the hormones, any changes to my body would evaporate and return to their original male yuckiness. Depressing as it was, I just did not have the money to continue buying hormones.

∼

Fast-forward to 2018. Strangely, I wasn't nervous, scared, or anxious as Shiona, the medical assistant sat me down in my new doctor's examination room. Shiona has a positive personality that would make you feel comfortable no matter what the dire circumstance. The practice, owned by Dr. David Lyter, Diversity Health Center of Tampa Bay, caters to the LGBTQ+ community. I had heard amazing things about Dr. Lyter. I was so ready to begin a legitimate HRT program. I had already submitted my letter of affirmation from my therapist, confirming that I am a candidate for hormone treatment. Dr. Lyter had Shiona perform a blood draw the previous week to get a baseline on my blood counts, and in particular, my hormone levels.

> No. I don't want it to work. And "it" should be an innie, not an outie.

It wasn't until I began this process that I realized just how many people that graduated high school and college didn't know both men and women have both sex hormones, just in different quantities. I had stupid amounts of testosterone circulating in my deformed male body. Before prescribing anything to me, he asked me two simple, yet important questions.

"Before we proceed, I need to understand your intentions on a couple of things," he said, "I don't expect you to answer these questions today. I'd like you to think each of them through for a bit. Ready?"

"Yes," I said excitedly.

"Okay. First. Do you still want IT to work?" He asked, as he motioned that he was speaking about my undesired private area. "And are you planning on having vaginoplasty? You know, Gender Confirmation Surgery. GCS? And please, take your time before answering. We can have another appointment after you've had time to consider these questions, and you can give me an answer then."

"Thank you. But I have to tell you something," I quickly responded.

"What's that?"

"No. I don't want *it* to work. And 'it' should be *an innie, not an outie.*" We both smiled at my metaphoric humor on the subject.

"I've thought this through for several decades. So, um, no," I said with a humorous inflection. "I don't need a second, let alone a week to tell you that."

"Okay. I just need to be sure before I prescribe anything," he replied. "Just understand this is a lengthy process that will involve years of changes."

We both stood up as he smiled and said, "Now. Let's get started, shall we?"

To my surprise, he prescribed the exact medications and quantities that I had purchased when I was foolishly self-administering mail-order hormones on and off over the past couple decades. "I'm finally doing things the right way, and safely." I thought with a sense of unparalleled self-accomplishment.

HRT was and is a delicate process. We had to get my testosterone lowered and under control to benefit from estrogen therapy. My testosterone had come back at 660 ng/dl. Just for clarification, that number is high. Like, I could literally get someone pregnant just by looking at them, high. But within less than two months Dr. Lyter had my testosterone levels down below 20 ng/dl, which is even lower than many cisgender women. As my doses slowly increased, so did my estradiol levels.

Within weeks I was beginning my *second puberty*. Now there's a phrase fewer than 1 percent of the entire human population will ever get to experience. I was now part of that statistic, and feeling ecstatic. Over the course of the next nine months, my progress, while slow, was definitely pleasing. My skin was softer. The hair on my arms seemed to be disappearing. My body fat was redistributing. I was getting a tummy or pouch as opposed to the "gut" men typically have. My face was becoming much dryer and needed more moisturizer each day. My "girls" were sore and definitely making their presence known. Then there were the changes in mood and emotion. Okay. Let's not go there. But what struck me more than anything else was that my voice was slowly changing. During one of my visits, I asked Dr. Lyter how this could happen. I already knew how that part of my anatomy was structured and permanently damaged.

We both concluded that much of my voice change was likely psychosomatic. I was unconsciously and naturally altering my voice.

During male-oriented puberty, the larynx grows, and the vocal cords (or more properly called, the vocal folds) become longer and thicker, thus making the person's voice deeper. These changes are all caused by testosterone and irreversible without intervention. For a little perspective, my voice was deep; like very, very deep. My voice had such deep rich character that it had me doing local and then national voice-over work for concerts. For context, I had the expected voice you would hear on a radio spot announcing a rock concert or Monster Jam. The movie trailer voice. My voice was similar to a very well-known country music artist I worked with, Josh Turner. If you don't know him, look him up and you'll get the idea. My voice now is the polar opposite of that. My voice has changed, not only in pitch, but in cadence, inflection, and intonation. My voice used to reside around B1 to E1 on a piano keyboard. Now it hovers around G#3 to B3; just below Middle C. I spent only a few months in voice therapy to retrain my voice. Now, where I speak is my natural speaking voice. In other words, I'm not "making" it go there. It now naturally resides there.

⁓

I often say to myself, "If I was a pre-teen today, I would have a great deal of help and support that didn't exist when I was a child. I could ask to be put on puberty blockers, then at the right time, introduce a similar hormone regimen that all of my girlfriends had naturally during their puberty."

It is sad when I see so much ignorance, especially in America, concerning my part of the population. Certain political leanings always trying to legislate against allowing transgender teens from getting the help they desperately need! The vast majority have incredibly positive outcomes and flourish in their lives. A superb example of how girls like me can be saved by puberty blockers and subsequent hormone administration is an amazing German recording artist named Kim Petras. Go look her up on YouTube.com. She didn't have to experience puberty the wrong way and thus avoided years of painful procedures and a few surgeries attempting to correct the permanent damage testosterone caused. But mostly, she avoided the real prospect of suicide. Look at some of Kim's videos. Yeah, she really looks like a very sad, depressed person, doesn't she? She is a wonderful example of what can happen for those of us that don't have to endure puberty the wrong way.

Okay. Go look her up now. I'll make it easy for you. For a great example, watch one of her music videos. It's a song named, "Heart to Break." And, don't worry, I'll be here when you get back.

Okay. Hold on. That was entirely too fast. You totally didn't watch the video, did you? Okay, here's the deal. I'm not allowing you to read a single word more until you go watch that video. Then, when you really get back, we can continue by going back a few years.

It's time I gave you some deeper perspective by showing you some crazy but amazing experiences that helped me get through this mess called me.

What Happens in Vegas
(apparently ends up here)

"I need you to go to Las Vegas with me in three weeks," Kirk said.
"You know me, Kirk. As always, I'm good to go. Thanks," I replied with excitement.

This would be my third trip to Las Vegas with the company. During each trip to Vegas, I would strategically carve out some free time for myself to meet up with one or more individuals just like myself that were transitioning or already fully transitioned. Still incredibly terrified to jump into the water myself, I remained in *boy mode*. I figured I could learn from others how to overcome my societal fears.

Shortly after our arrival at the Las Vegas Hilton and Convention Center, we met up with the show management team. In particular, there were two individuals that I was excited to see. I had worked with these two on a few past shows and needed to give them each a huge hug.

Their names, Julian and Robert. Both, very handsome men and an adorable happily "married" couple of eight years. Unfortunately, same-sex marriage had not yet been legalized when they celebrated their own private ceremony in Southern California.

It was typical with at least this show management company, that we would all get together for dinner and drinks on the first night. The owner of the Stratosphere had comp'd us a thousand dollars for dinner and drinks in the Top of the World restaurant at the top of the towering iconic hotel. With one of the six unable to attend, we all delighted in knowing we would certainly not waste a penny of the full offer.

Kirk and I were already seated when the rest of the party arrived. Upon Robert and Julian's arrival, Julian did a quick introduction of their plus-one guest, "Guys. This is Eric. Eric, this is Kirk and Eddie."

Eric was an amazingly handsome Latino man in his early to mid-30s. He had short dark hair, shaved on the sides, an amazingly symmetrical face with an expertly groomed five-o'clock shadow—the look I found most attractive in a man. Within a second of his arrival, I had already measured him up to be about 5'10" and possibly 170 pounds with what appeared to be a finely chiseled athletic build.

After a few glasses of wine, and before dinner had even arrived, my inhibitions had all left the building. I couldn't stop sneaking in several short gazes at him. I began asking Eric more about himself while the others continued a separate conversation.

"Do you live here in Vegas?" I inquired.

"No. Actually I live just outside Los Angeles. I've been there since I was a little boy. My family immigrated to America from Argentina when I was in the fifth grade."

"Do you work with Julian and Robert?" I continued.

"Ha. No. I actually work at an Argentinean Bistro near Venice Beach."

"Are you a chef?"

"Not yet. But hopefully soon. I'm currently the restaurant's sous-chef, which basically means, the second chef."

"Wow. That's *very* impressive. I've always loved to cook. I'm not in any league close to what you do, but I love to spice-up old recipes with my own freshness," I explained.

"Hmmm. Now, *that's* impressive. We should talk more about our love for food this week," he countered.

"I'd love that. So you came along with them to Vegas because who can refuse Vegas? Am I right?"

With a brief smile, he responded, "Yeah. Something like that, I suppose. Actually I really came just to see what these two *tontos* do when they say they work," as he looked across the table at Julian and Robert with a hint of playful sarcasm.

"Tontos?" Not knowing much Spanish.

"Yeah. In English it's like saying 'dummies'." He laughed.

Julian quickly broke in, "Come on Eric. Primo, tu sades que eres una estrella."

"Caramba, now everyone here knows I'm your cousin and yes cousin, compared to you, I suppose I am a star," he responded with a bullish pride.

"You guys are totally messing with me with the mixing of English and Spanish all at once aren't you?"

"Yeah. Just a little. It's just our thing. You know?" Eric explained.

"So what was Julian saying in that last exchange?" I continued asking.

"Oh. Nothing really. He was just saying, 'Cousin, you know you're a star.' To which I basically said *caramba,* which means, good grief."

I looked directly at Eric and said, "Ahhh. It's okay. I think you guys are so funny."

Shortly following dinner and sufficiently inebriated, we all decided to make our way to the Debbie Reynolds Hotel to watch Kenny Kerr perform his female impersonation drag show. If you've never heard, Kenny Kerr was by far the best female impersonator in Vegas; not a very good vocalist but could pull off brilliant impersonations of Cher, Barbra Streisand, and even Debbie Reynolds herself.

Kirk, visibly tired, said, "I'm going to pass guys. I'll see you all tomorrow morning at seven. Enjoy the rest of the night."

I wasn't about to pass up this opportunity, so I continued along with the other three on the half-mile walk to the hotel. We entered the hotel and proceeded to the gorgeous, very red themed theater. Kenny was already performing as we all took our seats at a table remarkably close to the stage. Of course, a bar tab was immediately started, courtesy of Robert and his company card. After what seemed to be several shots and drinks, Robert and Julian excused themselves from the table during a break in the performance.

"We'll be back in ten minutes or so. Don't do anything *we wouldn't do*." Julian sang rather whimsically while winking at his cousin Eric.

There I was sitting right next to him, this amazing specimen of a man. I just could not keep my eyes off of him. But based on what Julian just said, I wondered if they all had *clocked* my optical advances on Eric. That was when Eric began a more formal inquiry into my life.

"So do you have someone back home?" Eric asked, seeming to be heading into more formal inquiries.

"Not at present. No."

"May I ask you another rather personal question?"

Now incredibly nervous about the next question, I lightly cleared my throat and responded, "Sure. Ask away."

"Are you," he paused. "Are you gay? I don't typically need to ask, but unless I'm totally off-base, which doesn't happen often, you have been giving me *signals* all night. But I have to admit, you're a bit difficult to read. I mean I've noticed the way you've been looking at me all night. Am I right?"

Completely mortified that he was all over my gazes, I, with a hint of flirtatiousness, quickly and unexpectedly admitted, "Okay. Wow." I took a very visible deep breath and continued "Yes, I've been looking at you. And No. I'm not gay. *But*, I am different. Maybe that's what makes me *so difficult* to read."

Looking rather confused with my response he asked, "Different? What does that mean exactly?"

What Happens in Vegas (apparently ends up here)

"Yeah. So this is really hard for me to explain, so please don't tell the guys a word of this when they come back okay? *Please.*" I begged.

"Of course. Go on," he reassured.

"This may sound a bit strange to you, but by the time I was four years old, I knew..." I paused out of utter terror, then continued, "I knew I was a girl. But somehow I managed to fuck up my entry into this world and came out like this." I seemed to divulge my hidden truth within a single breath along with a slight, nervous laugh.

Eric lightly laughed along. He seemed impressed with my ability to say something so intimate and still throw in a sense of humor.

"So, my first intimate relationship was with a guy; a classmate, when I was thirteen years old. I loved him. But he hurt me both physically and emotionally. So I made it a point to only date women ever since."

"So hold on. Wait a minute. What I'm hearing you say is you're attracted to guys, but date women because you're too scared to come out as trans?"

"No. Not exactly. You don't underst..." I began as Eric interrupted.

"No. I do understand. I get it. You are telling me that you're a heterosexual woman pretending to be a lesbian, but still in boy mode. Am I right?"

I was absolutely blown away by his observation. I had never thought of my orientation in quite that way before. But his description was nothing short of brilliant. And how does he know so much about this stuff?

"Yeah. That's a great way to say it. Wow. You're good." I complimented.

"And what of this pendejo; this idiot? What happened to him?"

"One day, at lunch, he walked over to me and beat me up for no reason I could understand. We never had closure. I haven't spoken to him since. I never did find out why he did what he did."

Eric looked directly into my eyes and declared, "Listen. I like you," while simultaneously moving in a bit closer.

"Well, based on my completely obvious staring, I like you too. I'm just a little . . . " again Eric interrupted, but this time with a kiss.

There we were, embraced in a rather long, soft kiss. The butterflies I hadn't felt since Aaron so many years ago, suddenly reanimated, but a million times stronger. I placed my hand on his left cheek and kissed him back. All the while this amazing *thing* was occurring, I could not stop thinking about what this beautiful man saw in *me*.

"He's obviously gay," I thought. "So why would he kiss me after what I just said?"

But it was clearly evident that none of that really mattered. I was already completely involved in the moment and loving every last bit of it. Just as our lips parted, I looked up and saw Robert and Julian returning, and only a few steps from the table.

"Oh my God, I am so caught. Shit!" I thought.

"Mira los pajaritos del amor!" Julian declared with a huge smile.

"*Wow. Impressive. You guys!*" Robert added, nodding in agreement.

Frantically looking back at Eric, I asked, "What did he just say?"

"Well. Ah. Well, he just said . . . "

Julian interrupted and instead, gave the translation himself, "I said, look at you two love birds."

Then Robert chimed in with a whimsical flow, "You two are either really drunk or totally hot for each other. *My bet's on the second!* Oh, and by the way, *we saw the whole thing*. Very hot stuff my sneaky little mijos."

Completely embarrassed, I looked at Eric to say something in response. But instead, and without hesitation, he quickly leaned in once more and kissed me again. His advances were so intoxicating, I just went with it and kissed him back.

Eric looked up as if he were solving a problem then looked again into my eyes and declared, "Nope. I'm not drunk? So I vote for the second also."

What Happens in Vegas (apparently ends up here)

"Okay, everyone. One more drink before we leave. A toast to the two of you." Glasses clanged, then he finished with a smile and a wink, "y para un final agradable de tu noche."

Once more, I turned to Eric for another translation, "He was telling us to have a pleasant ending to our night. *If* you understand his context."

~

About thirty minutes later, 2 a.m. to be exact, we were all back at the Hilton and on-board the elevator to the floor show management had reserved. Julian and Robert's room was the first door on the left, only a few feet from the elevator.

With his usual flair, Julian said, "Good night you two. Make sure you sleep at some point. Okay?"

Eric's room, just a few more doors down the hall, was next.

"Want to come in for a few minutes?"

"Oh, my God. You are trouble. You are *definitely*—trouble." I revealed.

"Me, trouble? Maybe just a little," he admitted as he softly kissed me again while opening his door leading us inside.

Immediately, we were on the bed disrobing.

"I can't believe this is actually happening!" I thought almost out loud.

After all, this would be only the second guy to ever make love to me and really the first time as an adult. The anticipation was electric. Kissing and playing with him felt far more natural than with any woman I had ever been with. The wild butterflies. The racing heart. The internal, "take me" mechanism at full throttle. I had only one condition—that he does not touch me *there*. I didn't like any focus on that part of my anatomy. He quickly accepted my condition. And with his deep brown eyes, filled with unbridled intensity, fixed on mine just below him, he continued.

Even with his intoxicating intensity, he remained very gentle and hyper-focused on *my* pleasure as we made love over the next hour before passing out. Before long, the morning was already upon us, and with less than two hours of sleep, I knew I had to get out of his bed, get back to my room, and get ready for the day in short order. I slowly unwrapped his arm from around my midsection, gave him a gentle kiss on his cheek as he continued to sleep, then exited the room.

Of course the dynamic duo, Julian and Robert were armed and ready to get the juicy details from me, knowing full well Eric would not be in today.

"So? Did you make it to your room last night or did you find other accommodations?" Julian asked while cutely bumping my side.

"Yeah. About that. Can we please keep this out of the view of Kirk? *Please.*" I once again found myself pleading.

"Of course honey. Your secret is safe with us."

"Yes. I found other accommodations. But that's all I'm going to say. I ain't talkin'. Now. I need to find coffee!"

For the next six nights, we would all have dinner together, at a different elegant restaurant. While Kirk was around, I made sure Eric and I were not *too friendly*. Then after returning to the hotel each night, we would split off from the rest, quietly making our exit after a few drinks, hoping to slip out unnoticed in the crowd at the hotel bar. If we were missed, Kirk would just think we just went off to play some slots or Blackjack. I also knew Julian and Robert had my back too. Each night played out like the last.

After just two days, I felt like he was my significant other. We were playful, passionate, and enjoying each other while it lasted. The last evening in Vegas was rather difficult for me. I knew this would likely be the last time I'd see him for a while or possibly ever.

Although Eric's flight was not until 1 p.m., I had an 8 a.m. flight out of McCarran International to Newark, New Jersey. That meant checking-out of the hotel by 5:30 a.m. Spending the entire last night with Eric would be difficult, if not a gamble if I was to get out by five-thirty. But, as soon as we got away from everyone for the night, our plans began to evolve rather spontaneously. I couldn't recall another time in my life that I had ever kissed someone this much and for so long. We didn't sleep a wink that night.

"I want to stay up with you all night. I mean, I can sleep on the four-hour flight home instead," I said.

"Deal. By the way, I feel kind of ashamed that I didn't ask you this on that first day but, what is your name, *really*?"

In shock, as this was the first time this question had ever been asked of me, I immediately began to well up, then replied, "Amber. Amber Rose."

"That's a beautiful name. So where does Amber Rose come from? Like, how did that become your name?"

"It's word-play with my middle name really. My middle name is Ambrose. God, I hated that name. I mean, okay, it was my grandfather's name, but still. It was terrible. I believe I was about eight years old when I was playing with the sound of it. I would say Ambrose, again and again, while each time, saying it slower and slower, until, all by itself it morphed to two names, Amber Rose. I had no idea what 'Amber' was, but my mom's middle name is Rose and I found that middle name to be the prettiest name I ever heard. So really I changed both my first name and middle name all at once."

"That's a great story. Do you have plans to transition?" he asked carefully.

"I've had intentions to transition for my entire life. It's been so difficult. Every time I think I have amassed the courage to go through the process, something major happens in my life. Let's just say I've made a lot of mistakes that turned out to be life-changing events. I'm very happy they happened though. But that's a conversation for another time perhaps. But regarding transitioning, I have been kind of self-medicating with mail order hormones on and off for several years now."

"Ahhh. So that must be why you have those two cute teepees and amazingly large nipples," he said playfully.

"Yeppers. That would be the reason. But I really need to see an endocrinologist soon, so I can be monitored and make sure I'm on the right dosages."

"Good for you Amber. I hope that someday soon you finally get to live your truth." He whispered as he began to kiss me again. "I love your blue eyes, Amber."

I could not hold in the emotion of this moment any longer. I burst into tears and said, "No one has ever called me by my name before. You're the first one and I am happy it was you. You're amazing Eric. This week has really affected me and I know this will probably sound crazy to you, but after I'm back in New York, it's going to be hard to think about what I'm going to do without seeing you."

"Hey. Shhh. Chica. We'll stay in touch for sure, okay?"

Then looking at his entire incredible physique, I admitted, "I mean damn boy! I'm never going to forget this trip for real," as my tears began to transform into a subdued giggle. That giggle was just enough to serve as the prelude to him kissing me in fast short bursts while teasing me closer and closer to the bed for one last evening of playfulness and intimacy.

Mom's Final Wish

I was sitting in a surprisingly comfortable hospital chair at the foot of the bed where Mom was resting. I had been sitting there for about an hour with Dad. I watched him closely as he stood over her. The sound of the heart monitor as it made the *beep-beep* sound for each heartbeat was troubling to me. Mom was once again experiencing atrial fibrillation and tachycardia. Her heartbeat was so fast, and sounded like it was fluttering and skipping beats at the same time.

A nurse came in and took more vitals, before administering a drug through Mom's IV to help slow her heart rate. She then administered another medication to help lower her blood pressure. The nurse, named Jennifer, and a dear friend to the family looked at me and saw my concern for Mom.

"We'll make sure your mom is okay as fast as possible," she said reassuringly. Then she looked at Mom, whom she knew well from previous visits, and said in a humorous voice, "We don't want you here, Peggy. So let's break you outta here quick this time. Okay, hun?"

After the nurse left the room, Dad gave Mom a kiss on her forehead then turned to me and asked if I wanted anything from the cafeteria.

"No thanks, Dad. You go get some food. I'll watch over Mom."

Just after he left, Mom looked over at me and began crying.

"Aww, Mom, I'm right here. I love you. You're going to be okay. So don't worry."

"Honey?" Mom whispered. "Come here. I need to tell you something."

I quickly stood up and walked over to her bed and said, "I'm right here Mom," as I stroked my hand through her hair.

"Is your Dad gone?" she asked. "Yeah. He's probably halfway to the cafeteria by now."

"I need you to listen to me, honey," she said with a visceral intensity. "I'm going to die and ... "

I immediately interrupted her and assured her, "You're not going to die, Mom. They just gave you medicine to help you. I'm looking at your monitor right now and your heart rate is already coming down."

"Shhh!" she said as if annoyed. "Listen to me, please."

Standing over her and seeing her in such a terrible condition made it nearly impossible to fight off the tears I had been amassing.

"I *am* going to die, honey. And I want you to know something," she said as she welled up. Then she asked an unexpected question. "Do you still have *the issue*?"

"Mom? Come on. Let's not talk about that. Let's focus on getting you better so you can go home. Okay?"

Unsatisfied, she reasserted, "Do you *still* have *the issue*? Answer me."

For someone in her condition, she was still very much in the role of mom; a mom demanding answers on her terms. I sighed. I didn't want to tell her anything about *the issue*. It just didn't seem like the right time or place, and I already knew in my heart she would not be dying today. But her eyes kept piercing through me, not with disdain, rather with concern and unconditional love. Her eyes begged for an answer no matter what it was.

"Yes, Mom. It's not something that ever goes away, you know," I replied looking directly into her eyes.

"I see," she replied. "Is it any easier now that you're older? Tell me."

"Oh, Mom, please." I paused with a dreadful sigh. "No. It's far worse. But don't worry. I'm okay."

"You're *not* okay. You're a mess! You keep making mistakes with these women you pick up with. You marry them, have kids, then get divorced. You need to stop. This long show you've been performing is going to kill you. You might fool some people, but you can't fool your mother," she paused. "Can you hand me my water? I need a sip," then she continued, "Maybe it's time you just be that person? Just be who you told me you were when you were little. She's still in there, isn't she?"

I cried softly, "Yes."

"So stop all of this; whatever *this* is and be happy. Will you promise me that?" She continued crying tears of concern along with me. "I know I don't understand this thing you've been going through, but I know you can't keep doing what you're doing," she explained as if she was angry at God for putting me through this lifelong struggle.

"Just promise me you'll be safe. I've always wanted you to be happy and I've always known you're not."

With my left hand still stroking her soft, dyed, and graying auburn hair, I gave her a kiss on her forehead and I told her I would.

"Mom? First, you're not dying. Not tonight. And second. You're an unbelievably great mom. I want you to know how much I've always loved you. Knowing about my struggle for nearly my entire life had to be difficult for you to digest. But you've been my greatest protector and there's no one on this Earth I love more than you."

We had us a good cry, Mom and I. And just at that moment, Dad returned from his dinner break.

I needed to get home, so I leaned over Mom and gave her a great big cheek kiss, then put my cheek to hers. "I love you, Mom. I'll be back first thing in the morning."

Hiding From Myself

Mom gave me *the look*. The look that says, *don't forget what I just told you.* That was only maybe a year, before Mom first began showing definitive signs of early-onset Alzheimer's disease.

~

Six years later. "Eddie. It's Dad. You need to come to Fort Myers. Mom's deteriorating." There were very few times in my life I had ever heard my dad so emotionally distraught, and this was by far, the most distraught I had ever heard him. I packed up my things from work, told everyone what was happening, and headed home to get a bag packed.

I arrived at the adult care center where Mom had been living for the past half-year. Dad met me in the hallway to let me know she's slowly shutting down.

"How long, Dad?"

"They said, it could be fast, like a day or two, or it could be longer, depending on the fight within her."

I walked up to the bed and looked down at her. She was so emaciated. Her face had sunken in and presented pale gray, as if she had aged twenty-five years since the last time I saw her, which was only a few weeks earlier during Christmas. She was in and out of consciousness. Her lips were dry and severely chapped.

My sister called and said she would fly in from New York by tomorrow. I was happy we were all going to be there with her. "Mom, it's Eddie. I'm right here, okay. I love you. Colleen just called and said she's on her way too," I explained. The nurse came in and I asked, "Do you have any ChapStick or something we can put on her lips so they don't continue to dry out and crack?"

I just wanted Mom to be as comfortable as possible as the inevitable process slowly continued.

Colleen arrived the next day. Dad and I were so relieved she could get there so quickly. For the next four days, we sat with Mom all day until it was time to leave for the evening.

January 16, 2017

On the fifth day, Mom's breathing became more and more labored and I noticed her tongue was turning black. She would frequently moan as if in pain. She could no longer speak.

I sat on the right side of her bed and played her favorite songs; "This Guy's in Love with You" by Herb Alpert, "Chances Are" by Johnny Mathis, and "Let There be Peace on Earth", the Vince Gill version.

The nurse was now coming in knowing that Mom would begin mottling shortly. She told us to watch for color changes in her feet and legs. Mottling is a process where the body stops sending blood to organs not vital to your survival. So typically circulation will slow, then stop in the extremities and work its way up toward the vital organs, which are the last to shut down during this process.

Mom's eyes were open. She was looking directly at me. I had not seen that look in her eyes in over five years. She saw me. She recognized me. Mom was back. A woman dying from full-blown Alzheimer's was looking at me with a recognizable look. And that's when I heard her. Although she couldn't speak, she somehow talked directly to me, through with her eyes.

"Why isn't anyone trying to fix me?" I heard. She was crying as she spoke this through her eyes.

Mom's bouts with respiratory distress were getting worse, so I asked the nurse to supply her with morphine or anything they had that could help mitigate this. By late afternoon, I knew it would not be much longer. I stayed as close as I could to her, just softly talking to her and reminding her we were all with her. I even called her sister, my Aunt Kathleen, to allow her to say goodbye and give her a kiss from afar.

Then—the mottling began. It didn't take long at all for most of her extremities to shut down and blacken. Her breathing was slowing drastically. I looked over to Dad and softly motioned that it was time. Colleen, incredibly upset on the left side of Mom and me positioned on the right side of her, each had one of her hands in ours.

I felt compelled to talk her through the process. She was always so afraid of dying.

"It's okay, Mom. You can go. We love you so much! And I promise you we will all be together. I promise. We are already there with you." I softly preached to her.

I had always held the belief that if there is an afterlife and we are to believe that there is no beginning and no end in the afterlife, then one must conclude that we are both here and there simultaneously. As Colleen, Dad, and I were telling her how much we love her, I said to her several times, "I'm so proud of you." I was unsure of where those words came, but I said them a few more times. Then we experienced her final breath—a slow exhale. Mom, whose hands were limp the past five days, suddenly squeezed both Colleen's and my hands with impressive strength, then released. It was as if that was her final way to tell us she loves us. Then, her eyes gently closed all by themselves. Knowing she could still hear me for a few minutes longer, as it is widely thought that the last sense to go is hearing, I kissed her forehead and repeated how much I loved her several times over.

There are moments in one's life that define you; that change you forever. And I just experienced the biggest one of my life.

～

Mom loved the song, "This Guy's in Love with You" by Herb Alpert. It was one of the last songs she heard before passing. When I found out Herb Alpert was coming to Clearwater with his wife for a performance at The Capitol Theatre on May 6, 2017, I just could not let the moment pass without meeting him. I needed to let him know of this wonderful woman; my mom, that had just passed, and how much she adored his music.

I looked up the name of his management group in California and came up with just the person I needed to talk to. Xander. I called his office, knowing he would not be available, because that's how the music business works. I told his secretary who I was, and that I was also in the business. I also dropped a few names she would know just in case. I told her I needed to speak to Xander about meeting Herb for a few minutes while he was going to be in town.

In less than three hours, Xander returned my call. He said, "Listen. I want to help you, but Herb and his wife don't really do meet and greets anymore."

"Oh. This is really not a meet and greet, Xander." I said, "I know how things are, but this would mean a lot. As a songwriter who has been in the business for twenty-six years, I want to let him know how grateful I am for one particular song that my mom loved. In fact, it was the last song she listened to before she passed just a few months ago from Alzheimer's."

"I will ask Herb right now and call you back *in ten* okay. I think he might make an exception for you, but let's wait and find out. I'll do what I can for you."

Five minutes later, Xander called back and said, "Herb said he would be delighted to meet after the show."

"Xander. Thanks. I appreciate you looking into this for me." I replied.

The night of the show, Herb, his wife, and his band put on an amazing show. I marveled as this legend who co-founded A&M records so many years ago, performed so gracefully at the age of eighty-two. He easily appeared twenty years younger.

After waiting for the theatre to clear out and showing security my credentials, I waited by the stage and called Xander. A few minutes later he and I walked into what I was all too familiar with; a small room with fold-up chairs and a table that held two boxes of cheese pizza and a bottle of Coke. Herb walked in, and we all introduced ourselves.

Out of all the famous people I had met in my life, this was the first and only time I ever became *starstruck*. There he was. This brilliant, talented, lovely man and billionaire that I admired, not only for his genius but because of my mom's love for his music. During our introductions, we began talking about the business a little, when I chimed in and told him how amazing his sculptures were.

That single statement gave Herb incredible pause. "You know something. I've been on tour for a long time and no one has ever brought up my sculptures, let alone told me how amazing they are. I like you," he said with a pat on my back. "I'm happy you like them and know of them. They're my passion."

It was then that I told him about Mom and how much she loved that one song, and how it was one of the last songs she heard before passing just four short months ago. The conversation quickly turned emotional as both of us spoke about each other's tragic experiences with Alzheimer's disease and the pain of watching someone you love slowly disappear right before your eyes. Thank you, Herb.

Twin Flame

A few years before Mom's passing, I experienced something and someone so incredible, I am still affected to this day. So let's step back a few years.

I pulled into the large parking lot of the two-story country nightclub about ten minutes early. This evening, I would meet Debbie and her friend Denise, who were on their way back from a Rascal Flatts concert. This was only my second date after signing divorce papers. A sign illuminated the side of the building that resembled an enormous barn you'd find on an industrial farm. It read, "Dallas Bull". Their claim; one of the largest honky-tonks east of the Mississippi. It was a mecca for country music fans because it was large enough to support concerts, yet small enough to get up close and personal. Although I had lived in Tampa for the past five years, this was the first time I ever went to this venue. I wondered to myself, "Why haven't I been here before?"

This was definitely my kind of place. I had spent so much time writing music in Nashville and New York, working alongside so many country music artists. As I got out of my car, I called Debbie to find out when she would be arriving.

"I'm here, standing by the front door with Denise," she responded loudly, trying to compensate for the loud live music coming from within the club.

"Ah. I'm walking towards you right now. See you in a sec." I countered.

I was strangely nervous. I've been quite the extrovert for many years and rarely had even a glimmer of nervousness when meeting someone. This, the first time I would meet Debbie in person, had me feeling like a teenager going on their first date. I had seen several photos of her, but that did not prepare me for my first glimpse in-person. Taking everything in within only a single moment, I memorized her. She was stunning. Her long blonde hair draped around her and came to rest just below the top of her blouse. Her face defied her age by over ten years—easily. And her eyes were a beautiful green hue.

While introducing myself to her friend Denise, Debbie moved in and embraced me in a quick hug while saying, "You look very nice." After thanking her, I returned the compliment. While walking into the nightclub, she held my hand. I thought it was a wonderful gesture. She just had a way about her that from the first moments of being with her, put me at ease.

I surprised Denise by paying her cover and ours. Denise seemed shocked that I would do that for her. But I told her that where I'm from, and where I've been, this is how it works. I sensed I immediately earned bonus points with her.

This place was enormous. There were already hundreds of people inside. The focal point of the first floor was the stage at the opposite end of a sprawling room sporting a dance floor that could easily accommodate a hundred people. An up-and-coming country group from Nashville occupied the stage. The ceiling above this room was, in a word, spectacular. It spanned what appeared to be not two, but three stories. Then on every other wall of the enormous room, there were fully stocked bars that spanned the entire lengths of each wall.

Our first stop was to get some drinks at the nearest bar. Denise made her way back to the entrance as her date arrived. When she returned, we did casual introductions while the band took their first break. Coincidentally, the DJ began playing a Rascal Flatts song, "Bless the Broken Road." So without hesitation, I looked directly into her eyes, took the drink from her hand, and then looking at Denise and her date, I commented, "Please excuse us, we have a date out there," as I pointed at the vacant dance floor.

She seemed surprised that I did this. It was all over her face. Something that silently spoke, "Oh My God. Oh, he's good. He's really good."

As we danced, I quickly glanced around the room as hundreds of others watched us. From that moment forward, it was just me and her. No one else existed. In my periphery, I could see the other women telling their dates or boyfriends to follow our lead and get on the dance floor. There was something already happening between us. It was like nothing I ever felt before. It was electric. The way she looked up at me and the way I looked at her made my heart swirl. My heart hadn't swirled like that in a very long time. In fact, the last time that happened was with Eric in Vegas. At the end of the song, I dipped her, and as she slowly rose back up, I greeted her with a light kiss.

Upon returning to our table, she and Denise made their way to the ladies' room while I stood awkwardly with Denise's date. We didn't have a single word to say to each other. Nope. Nothin'. Or at least, he didn't care to talk to me. So I figured it was another case of a typical hot guy with an ego bigger than his . . .

Although Denise's date was clueless about what was transpiring in the ladies' room, I knew. Something incredible just happened between us on that dance floor. I knew when she returned, we would part ways with Denise and her date. Besides, it was beyond obvious to both of us we had a different agenda awaiting us. There was really no way to talk because the music was deafeningly loud. So we made our way upstairs to the next deck. The second deck was amazing all by itself. There were more bars, another slightly smaller dance floor, and a DJ playing dance and techno. We stood overlooking the country bar below when our eyes met again. We both leaned in and kissed. This was not just a kiss, mind you. This was "A Kiss." It was an explosion of crazy intensity when our lips met. Within seconds we were making out as if we were two college students hooking up. For at least the next two hours, we were completely immersed in multiple passionate make-out sessions.

"What is going on here?" I asked. "I can't get enough of you. I can't stop kissing you. This is amazing."

Even onlookers had that look. And not the look of, "Ew. Look at the two forty-somethings making out; totally gross." The looks were shouting, "Wow, you two are fucking hot!" And we were! Interestingly, never in my life had I ever made out with someone as long as I did her that night. No one. She was already something altogether new to me.

As the night grew later, we walked outside to give our tinnitus-stricken ears a rest. We found an empty bench just outside the front entrance where we made-out all over again. It was nearly 1 a.m. when Denise and her date found us in the middle of one of our sessions.

She said, "So, I'm going to head over to his place if that's okay, Debs? I'm sure you can get a ride back to the hotel, right?"

Debbie looked at me, and for the first time that evening, I didn't know what to say. I had no intention of being intimate with Debbie. But, I said, "I'll get her to the hotel. No worries, Denise."

Curious and a little lost about the current situation, I asked Debbie, "I thought you said you lived here in Tampa? Why do you need a hotel?"

"We always get a hotel if we're going out for an evening. It's safer, and I never said I lived in Tampa, silly. I live almost an hour from here."

Moments later, after what I considered being the best date of my life, I drove her back to her hotel. I parked the car, then walked over to her door and let her out so we could enjoy a proper goodnight kiss without the clumsiness of the car seats between us. Nearly forty-five minutes later we were still standing next to my car kissing.

During a brief break, I told her I would walk her to the lobby and then be on my way. As we entered the lobby, I walked her to the elevator and kissed her one last time as she got on. As the door was closing, I found myself inside the elevator with her, where we kissed yet again. I walked her to her room and declared with all the strength I could muster, "Okay. So this is where we need to say goodnight. I had an amazing time tonight. You are quite the kisser and it is hard for me to leave, but I have to go."

"I understand," she replied. "You're quite the amazing kisser too," she replied as her door slowly opened.

We both leaned in for one more small kiss, which became one of the best kisses of the evening. Everything was fireworks, like Gucci. I succumbed to the moment.

"Well, this is something new?" I thought ironically.

It was the strangest thing. I had gone through several girlfriends, and three wives, and never once had this level of attraction or emotion hit me. Never. I mean, I had feelings at the beginning of every relationship, but never this intense; and *this* wasn't even a relationship—yet.

Over the next few months, Debbie and I saw each other every chance we could. Our schedules were sometimes difficult to navigate. But when we came together, we were back to being two passionate college students enjoying their first love. It was such a new and wonderful feeling.

Then it happened. I knew I was in love. I loved everything about her. I even loved her crazy goodnight salutation, "Go home Kiddo." But the words that always hit me in the stomach were three words she would say to me. They were her words of affection and a hint to me I had already broken through a piece of her painful brick wall.

"You are trouble," she'd say.

"Interesting choice of words," I thought. The same words I had used several years ago with Eric.

"I am, aren't I." I'd reply with a mysterious grin. Then I would lean in and steal her lips with my own.

But every day, just like clockwork, the struggle that sentenced me to a lifetime of perpetual, annoying harassment would creep into the foreground of my thoughts.

"What are you doing? You can't do this! You've been here before so many times and you never learn." The argument would begin. "You're going to break her heart or doom this relationship just like you did three times before."

The longer this argument went on, and the stronger our relationship grew, the more conflicted I became.

"Do I just tell her? Do I let her in on who I am? Will she understand? How will my kids deal with all of this destruction I've had in my personal life?"

I was growing more and more anxious. I knew I was in love. But I just could not shake the thought I was merely repeating a vicious cycle of relationships, all sentenced to the death penalty, and affecting my kids because I was still hiding from myself. So I did what any conflicted asshole would do. I ghosted her and went back to my third ex-wife.

That's right. You heard me correctly. There's literally nothing more ridiculously brain-dead I could have done that would have surpassed the idiocy I had perpetrated. *That* was the only thing I could come up with at the time? Really? Truly, it mystifies me to this day.

Close to five years later, and long after diving back into a relationship that was worse than dating a starving Jeffrey Dahmer, I finally freed myself from the hell I submitted myself to. Remember when I said I was religiously agnostic? Well, my faith in God remains unshaken, regardless. God knew the road I was on, and while I didn't like it, he gave me a miracle. He gave me my youngest child, who has filled my life and heart with such an abundance of love and blessings, you'd think I *should* be religious. Although the marriage was—wait. Let's get this part correct, shall we? I wasn't in a marriage. If there is a hell, I was in it; like crossed the River Styx kind of stuff. I mean, we lived on separate sides of the house for nearly the entire time.

I spent all of those years hating myself for what I had done to Debbie. Not a single day passed, I didn't think of her. I say that literally, and I know exactly how it feels to not have a day go by without dwelling on my incongruity.

Underneath it all, there was a lesson finally being learned. It was a lesson that began three decades earlier with a wonderful girl named Karen. Everything was moving in on me fast. I often cried about what I had done to Karen nearly thirty years earlier. But also, crying because I had more recently sacrificed something that was brand new to me—an unfamiliar love. I had to live with the decisions I made that plagued my every thought nearly as much as my incongruity. But more so, I knew the time to face my demons had come. There was something big happening to me. It was as if I was awakening. The pain I was feeling was nearly five years old, but it may as well have happened five minutes ago.

I began speaking to a friend at USF Connect in Tampa who was an empath and spiritual advisor of sorts.

"These emotions and life changes you are experiencing come from the universe not-so-gently nudging you back onto the road from which you strayed so long ago," she said. "I feel such visceral pain inside of you, especially about Debbie. Have you spoken to her lately?"

"No. But I need to. I can't go on like this. I'm literally crying about it every day and it's been nearly five years! I probably need therapy."

"Honey, don't think me strange for saying this, but Debbie could be what we call, your *twin flame*."

I had never heard that term before, but I wanted to know what it meant. "What's a twin flame?" I asked.

"A twin flame is the other half of your soul. Don't confuse it with a soul mate. Basically, you and her are of the same spirit, and somehow you split into two distinct people—half of your spirit hers and half of her spirit yours. In my spiritual teachings, you share a common past with your twin flame. Each half of the twin flame always finds its counterpart, or other half, to teach very important lessons. My advice is to just go with the universe right now. Trust your gut, because your gut is your soul."

Although the road I was on seemed paved with brimstone, I was about to find out there was more to my life and troubles than I ever admitted or allowed myself to see.

Spiritual Awakening

I spent decades blaming the women I married for the marital troubles that always ensued and eventually led to divorce. I would say, "she cheated on me," or "she was emotionally and physically abusive to me." While these were all valid and truthful accusations, they didn't reveal the entire context of the situation that led to our demise. It wasn't until I had, what I call, a spiritual awakening, that I realized I was doing everything, and I mean everything in my life wrong. I had sensed it for quite some time, beginning with my revelations about Karen all those years ago. Now, after a more bitter and painful revelation that I ghosted the only woman that I had ever loved completely (Debbie, whom I still believe to be my twin flame) there was no denying it.

This awakening consumed me. It was slapping me across the face harder than the sub-zero wind I experienced every January growing up in upstate New York. Perhaps all I had experienced and learned so far in my life had finally coalesced; providing me with a new sense of understanding and a fresh perspective into myself and the world that surrounds me.

So many things were changing; my sense of humanity, humility, compassion, and empathy were all becoming more vivid and intense. I

Hiding From Myself

> Eddie was screwing up my entire life and the people that surrounded me. I couldn't permit him to drive any longer. I had to pull that car over and let him out.

innately knew I was finally ready to be honest with not only myself but the entire world that surrounded me. It was time to stop asking the annoying question, "When is my life going to start?" I realized I had not been living and instead was the pathetic understudy to the martyr in my own Shakespeare tragedy.

Before I could live, I had to break through decades of insecurity, fear, and self-imposed assimilation. I had to take off the mask I was wearing for so long. I had to bring myself into the reality that I was actually the causality behind the troubles I had always complained about. It was time to let go of Eddie. Eddie was screwing up my entire life and the people that surrounded me. I couldn't permit him to drive any longer. I had to pull that car over and let him out. Even though that metaphoric scene seems a bit cliché, to this day I can still see him in the rearview mirror while the distance between him and I expand ever further as I continue to drive away.

I wrote a quote after my spiritual awakening that sums up what I had to do to *awaken*.

> *"A true **spiritual awakening** is only possible once you've **released** your **eyes from seeing** and your **ego from defending**."*

Personally, I have a very deep connection with God. I understand that God is not the engendered "Him" we created some time ago. God is also not some mythological wizard that comes down and saves a little boy from leukemia and ignores the one next to him as he dies.

Spiritual Awakening

That's not the way this works. That's not the way any of this works. A genuine connection with God is one of an actual relationship. A relationship with no asks; just trust, faith, and love guiding us to the best versions of ourselves.

My spiritual metamorphosis has profoundly changed how I see myself and the world. To this day I still can't describe to anyone how it happened and why it coalesced on one particularly ordinary day while speaking with my friend at USF Connect.

She and I sat at a quiet high-top table in the enormous lobby talking about all things spiritual. She could sense so many things about me without me even speaking them out. Our past conversations about Debbie proved that to me.

"I sense so much conflict in you. Am I right?" she said.

I couldn't help but to let out a short laugh as her words seemed to materialize straight out of a *Star Wars* movie.

"Yes, actually," I responded nervously. I knew I was about to reveal to her who I really was. This was a gigantic step because she would be the first person I would tell my secret to in a very long time.

I began revealing my lifelong secret to her and the circumstances that put me where I was currently. I spent the next thirty minutes telling her everything I could about who I was.

"I am going to shock you, Eddie. I have always known you were different. The past couple of years I have known you, I always sensed it. So telling me these things are no great revelation to me. But I am honored that you value my friendship as much as you do. For you to open and reveal the most primal and intimate parts of who you are to me reinforces how I have always seen you."

As nervous as I was, my greatest truth was now out there beyond the confines of myself. This revelation of truth became the defining pivotal moment in my life. I had finally recognized that I could finally let go of my lifelong torment and release myself from my irrational fears, which almost always led to poor choices. I could free the person I had been imprisoning her entire life.

I knew where this would all eventually lead me, and for the first time in a long time, I was feeling a sense of exhilaration. I needed to go through all the various pieces of my life and scatter them out about the floor. Then one by one I could organize them into rational and objective collections of mistakes and triumphs. I needed to look carefully at each one, and humble myself before my mistakes, and smile at my triumphs. I had to admit to my very soul that while my intentions were well-intended, assimilating and conforming caused many of my life's most hurtful moments. When I began revisiting my life, I realized that it wasn't just about my wives' mistreating or cheating on me; it was about me pretending to fit into situations and relationships that I didn't belong in. I had convinced myself for so long that this was the only way I could live my incongruent, secret life.

It was too difficult to explain my sexual orientation to people. How does one explain that they are transgender and a woman while looking like a man? Further, how does one explain that they are **not** gay? And would people understand when I tell them I'm a heterosexual woman? People judge books by their covers almost always. It takes time for most to "get it."

I found myself, time and time again, doing the most unnatural things an incongruent person or any person can do. Since high school, I forced myself to be with women because there was no other way to be in a relationship safely. Even though it was a miserable failure every time, I didn't heed the warnings. I didn't learn from my obvious mistakes.

I had only one thing going for me. I ensured that I revealed who I was to each one of my wives before marriage. However, that information came with the revelation that there would be no conceivable way for me to transition. I told them I wished I was not born like this, but I am who I am. And you know what? They married me anyway.

Spiritual Awakening

So at the very least, I went into each marriage giving them my best attempt at an honest answer I could, given my misguided assimilation attempts.

Honestly, I was not a suitable husband for any of them. I didn't know how to be a husband. I would watch and study guys with the intensity of a law student studying for the Bar the night before the exam. I tried time and time again to imitate them, but it never worked. From someone else's vantage point, it appeared what I was doing was working. But from my side of things, it just wasn't. Let's also understand that admitting I was not a suitable husband doesn't mean I was a horrible person. It means that I just couldn't be the *man* that each of these women needed in their life. I still remember some comments from one of my ex-wives.

"You argue like a woman!"

"Why can't you just be a man? You're so weak!"

"I don't want to hear about your health problems. I'm not your mom! You're a pussy! You're not a real man!"

Interestingly, the person that said those words to me, to this day remains absolutely clueless to what it is to be transgender. In fact, I would say, this person is one of the most ignorant and bigoted people I know.

Regardless, at the time, I understood that everything said was true, (except "You're a pussy"). Deep down, part of me even thought I deserved to be verbally abused.

The truth along with some objective perspective came out after several therapy sessions. It was a resounding, flat-out, "No!"

"You don't deserve to be beaten up emotionally or otherwise just because you don't fit into someone else's tiny definition of what defines a man or a woman. No one has the right to treat you with that kind of disdain."

But through the decades of failed relationships and chaos, there was something I was grateful for. It was the life-changing experience of being a parent four times over. I had made a conscious decision long before I met any of my wives. Since I was born ill-equipped to bear children, I would give it my best effort to accept my position in life and attempt to move that life forward to having a family.

My four children have always been my greatest gift. I would not be here right now telling you this story if it wasn't for my four boys. They helped to transform a person who was once so despondent she wanted to leave this world, into a person who couldn't imagine her life without them in it. So would I do it all over again, just to ensure each one of them existed? You bet I would! Every time and twice on Sunday!

> It was time to free Amber. She—I, had no place to hide anymore.

The awakening had happened. There was no going back. I saw the world through a different lens now. And once you see the world through this lens, you can't unsee it. It's a magical revelation devoid of religious or political ideology. I knew this revelation had put me back on a path I fearfully departed a long time ago. It was time to take positive action in my life. It was time to free Amber. She—I, had no place to hide anymore. I had no more excuses. I needed to face the world with my newfound confidence, strength, humility, and authenticity and let it be known that this is me. This is who I have always been, and this is who I will always be. I had to say it unapologetically, but also with a great deal of patience, and possibly some thicker skin.

The Butterfly's First Flight

Let's cut to the chase. Coming out can be a genuine pain in the ass. Coming out starts out as an amazing rush that releases a lifetime of burden. It allows you to put forward a fresh revelation of your truth. A truth that you will share with people whom you love. That's a wonderful and liberating feeling. But the repetitive nature in which I approached it became exhausting.

As you will see, when I came out, I did so with the fury of a brigade of women fighting their way into Prada for the final remaining few handbags placed at 75 percent off—today only!

I told everyone I knew. I told my dad, my sister, my children, my exes, aunts, uncles, cousins, colleagues at work, and my friends (the ones from childhood to my most recent friends). At first, I did so personally. I didn't create the cliché impersonal one-size-fits-all post on Facebook while anxiously awaiting hundreds of likes and fake congratulatory comments and replies. Instead, I met the special people in my life in person or at the very least, called each one individually. Why go through all of that trouble, you ask?

For the answer, you first have to ask yourself two questions. Why am I coming out and why do I need to tell these people? Although the number of people you tell may differ, the answer to both questions is rather easy to understand. *These people* represent the people I love and care about; people important to me—whether I've known them my entire life or have only befriended them recently.

At least for my circumstances, I thought, if I was to reveal my authentic self, I needed to be 100 percent honest and transparent, and 200 percent patient. Both my approach and how I handled questions and feedback would be critical to my success. I had to do this perfectly, every time—possibly hundreds of times. I knew that many people would have absolutely no idea what I was even talking about. For some, it would be a total shock; something they didn't see coming. And for many others, the idea of someone being transgender had never even been broached. To them, transgender would still be a word without a clear and accurate definition. Then, there would be those who would have some mythological, religious objection that I would need to navigate. And still further, there was my family, and in particular my four children; my four boys, all at different ages and stages of their lives.

The complexity was real. I had to consider the way I would divulge this information to each of them in an appropriate, compassionate, and loving way. I had to get this right, and I had to be patient and empathetic to everyone's concerns should they arise. Although I had already lived an entire lifetime dealing with this, for them, this would all be brand new and possibly difficult to comprehend at first. For the vast majority of people, they only saw me as another guy for my entire life, and this conversation could easily turn this into, "He's having a midlife crisis moment."

When you are transgender, you spend a great deal of time, sometimes many years, trying to figure out the correct way to come out to different people. You do this while fighting your own subconscious demons and irrational fear. Don't discount that fear just because it's irrational—it's a bitch and it will attempt to ruin your life in nearly every way it can! It's powerful.

The Butterfly's First Flight

The fear of familial rejection, social isolation, and loss of employment are just a few of those fears. Add bullying, jeering, assault, and the possibility of being the victim of a hate-filled homicide and it becomes extremely difficult to even contemplate coming out, let alone, transitioning.

I grew up and lived most of my life in rural backwoods, *more deer than people*, small town, USA. Many of the people that lived in my upstate New York town, especially when I was a child, had a very limited understanding of diversity. The fear I had about my gender identity and my sexual orientation finally had me move from the area completely. I always knew I would need to escape that tiny town so I might have even the smallest chance of conquering my fears and becoming congruent one day.

It was several years later, while living in Tampa, Florida, that I finally was no longer capable of *faking* my life anymore. I was exhausted from asking the same question, again and again, year after year, "When is my life going to begin?" That question was actually far more existential than I had ever imagined. There was a scary, secret truth behind that question that required a much deeper and conscious understanding of not only my incongruity but how that incongruity would someday get resolved.

Either way, I needed to deal with it. I had allowed it to consume me for far too long, which I attribute to a slew of scary health-related problems accompanied by anxiety. It had been literally eating me alive, cell by cell, for my entire life. But more importantly, I needed to stop the backward process of continuous assimilation and conformity that I was failing to pull off without casualties. I needed to stop trying to be what I thought society wanted me to be. I needed to stop living in fear of the negative reactions I would get from some people after divulging and living my truth. I needed to stop doing the same things time and time again, expecting a different result, because all by itself, that one thing was the definition of crazy. To be technically accurate, the way I was dealing with—or hiding from myself—made me nuttier than a squirrel turd. I hate that that was me, but love that phrase.

It was definitely time to be strong, confident, and resolute. But above all, I had to stop hiding from myself and just be myself, and not the caricature of a person everyone knew. Now all I needed was a plan.

∽

I had gone through my fair share of psychologists since my early twenties. I remember my first session in Mahopac, NY. I traveled nearly one hundred miles each way just to keep this as private as possible. Besides, I knew most of the psychologists in my town, so that wasn't going to happen. He charged $80 per one-hour session. The bonus for me was when I asked if he could help me with my "living my life as the wrong sex" conundrum, he responded with an enthusiastic, "Yes." So I booked the appointment.

It took me three visits to figure out he didn't have the foggiest clue what I was talking about. I was paying him $80 an hour to educate him. Yeah, so that was that. Adios. Disappointed, I began to once again seek someone that could help me.

About one year later, I found another psychologist oddly in the same town of Mahopac. I called, but this time grilled the shit out of the guy before committing to driving that far and not charging *him* a consultation fee for educating him.

I grilled him on stuff I knew before I was even in high school. He answered all of my questions brilliantly. He seemed impressed that I was so well versed on the subject, to which I responded, "Yeah. You kind of become an expert on something when you *are* that something."

During my first couple of sessions, we went into how long this had been going on and the emotions and frustrations I felt. We talked about my near-fatal depression when I was fourteen. We talked for a substantial amount of time about my newborn son, Corey. He asked questions about my sexual orientation, my sex life, and cross-dressing.

"About cross-dressing," I refuted matter-of-factly, "I have known I was a girl since I was four years old. I came to you today in the clothing of a man, did I not?"

"Yes. Go on," he replied, as he readied himself for what was sure to be an attempt at a smartass remark.

"Well—I feel I am cross-dressing right now like this. In its purest sense and definition, one that I've been acutely aware of since the eighth grade, am I not doing just that right this very minute?"

He seemed bewildered and speechless by my rather *on-point* point. A point he revealed, he had never heard put quite that way before.

"When I wear women's clothing, I look horrible. I have serious damage from testosterone. So, to answer your question about cross-dressing correctly. Yes, I cross-dress, but not the way you have suggested, but the way I have just described."

By the end of the second session, he began talking to me about some questions he had been asking. "Many of the questions I have asked you were to complete an initial diagnosis. And some of your answers were more accurate than what this *DSM* describes." He paused as he flipped to a specific page.

"Eddie, you have something the *DSM* classifies as," and in near unison, we both gave the same diagnosis and phrasing. "Gender Identity Disorder," he then paused and said, "You impress me. You know the *DSM*, do you?"

"I'm pretty familiar with those pages within the *DSM*, yes."

"As we move forward, we may explore some things that can happen," he explained.

"I already know about hormone replacement therapy, sexual reassignment surgery, electrolysis, breast augmentation and many other things. The answer since I was a child was always a resounding yes to the entire painful process."

"After a few more sessions, I can recommend an endocrinologist that can administer hormones. Next session let's talk about the long-term effects of moving forward. And how it may affect you and your son."

That session never happened. My life was once again in a spinning cycle of madness. It would be over a decade before I would meet my current therapist here in St. Petersburg. I always looked forward to my weekly visits.

She was an amazing listener. In fact, so good, that she could easily recite the entire session back if asked. And trust me that's an amazing skill because honey I love to talk and talk and talk; ask anyone.

Although aware of my history and current circumstances, she kept our sessions focused on my children. I dedicated each session on how I would navigate and alter my narrative for each of them based on their age.

When you are transgender, you spend a great deal of time, sometimes many years, trying to figure out the correct way to come out to different people.

"I have been dwelling on and worrying about how I would tell my kids since the day each of them was born. How do I say the right things in a loving and nurturing way? A way they will understand? Will their generation just get it, or will they not understand at all?" I rambled on worriedly.

"I think it's wonderful that you've been thinking about this so thoughtfully and for so long. Consider the things you have already told me. The conversations with your boys in New York about diversity and acceptance. The conversations they had with you regarding their classmates at school. That they can speak to you so openly and comfortably about topics concerning people that are gay and/or transgender has already set that stage for you," she assured. She also complimented, "Hearing about your ex-wife, Christine, and how she has the same openness with the boys is amazing. These are all things that, when you are ready, will definitely guide your family discussion in a very positive direction."

I told her I had to begin the coming out process soon. So she compiled some articles on how to come out to family, friends, and coworkers. "Read the articles I will email to you. Then during our next session, we can begin discussing a plan and roadmap for your coming out process and create it on your terms. Sound okay?"

"This is wonderful, yes."

Not only did I read each article she forwarded to me, but I updated my list of important people within days. Before the week was over and before my next session, I had come out to two of my coworkers with overwhelming success and acceptance. It had a certain irony to it. The very thing that placed me in a deep sense of fear turned out to be hugely irrational.

I had prepared myself for the possibility of an exercise in WTF'isms. I didn't know what to expect but my determination to follow through was unshakable, damn the consequences. Over the next two weeks, I would come out to nearly eighty people. I knew I was a blessed individual because out of those eighty people, I had very little negativity. It was incredible; a total release of weight and fear brushed off of my shoulders almost effortlessly. That was when I knew most of the fear I harbored most of my adult life was irrational. All it took were those few words of affirmation from my new therapist to set some profound life-changing things in motion.

The Reveal

Apr 28, 2018: Dad

Filled with both excitement and fearful anticipation for what was to come later this evening, I pondered the thought. Am I coming out to Dad tonight or did Mom tell him years ago and he just never brought it up? And if she did tell him, does that mean he's far too uncomfortable to talk about it? But, if she didn't, will he even understand what I'm about to divulge to him? I was driving myself crazy with anticipation.

I made us a nice dinner before bringing him into the living room for "the talk". As nervous as I was, I knew I would be okay either way.

"Dad, I want to tell you something but I'm confused about where to start. So that said, I'm going to tell you something that you might already know. But I will tell you as if you don't know. So here we go."

"Have you ever heard of the word transgender?"

"No. I'm not sure I've ever heard that before?" he replied.

"Transgender is a term that describes someone whose gender identity doesn't match the sex they were assigned at birth. For a simple example, it's like a baby that was assigned male at birth that when they get a little older, don't identify male, but female. Their brain doesn't match their body. I am one of those examples and realized it at four years old."

"So you're gay? But you married women?" Dad replied.

"No. Okay let me clarify some of this for you. What you just described is someone's sexual orientation. That describes a romantic and/or sexual attraction to another person whether it is the opposite sex or the same sex, or both. Let's leave that one at that for now, because that rabbit hole goes a little deeper than I want to explain right now."

"What I am referring to is gender identity, which is one's sense of their own gender. So, to help, you are a man, and that is that. You've probably never asked yourself the following question a single time in your life. Why am I a male and not a female? You just always knew subconsciously you're a guy. End of discussion, right?"

"Okay. True."

"Think of it this way. Sexual orientation is who you go to bed *with*, and gender identity is who you go to bed *as*."

"My life has been complex, Dad. I am transgender. I have always identified as female. But I did what I had to do to conform to what everybody saw me as: a guy. I told Mom about this when I was four. Do you remember Mom telling you something like this, ever?"

"Your mom never told me anything like this. I have never heard this before."

It bewildered me. All those years and Mom never told Dad?

"Interesting," I replied.

For the next hour, I explained my lifelong struggle to Dad and attempted to answer his many questions. Dad was an important person in my life and I was nervous he was just not going to get it, or worse, possibly make up some odd reason for me going through all of this. But he didn't. Dad came through the other side of this awkward conversation with, "I love you. And that is that. You told me a lot of unfamiliar things tonight and it's going to take me a while to digest it all. But I know what you just told me, and I accept it."

Wow. Mom never told him and, wow, he is accepting of what I told him. Telling your family and having them reject you is something so many of us contend with. God blessed me with parents who loved their children unconditionally. Mom, my protector for so many years, never told Dad. And now Dad just made my spirit glow brighter than the sun.

Within months he was already describing me as his daughter, and when holidays came, the cards were always describing a daughter. That type of affirmation is exactly what every trans person dreams of. My dad so totally rocks! Don' cha' think?

May 20, 2018: Corey, my eldest son

"You are putting out the flags with us this year aren't you Corey?"

"Yes, of course."

"Good Papa and I will fly up the Wednesday before Memorial Day and be in town for a week. I have something I need to talk to you about. It's important."

"Why can't you just tell me now?"

"It's something I really need to do in person, okay."

"You're scaring me. Are you sick? You need to tell me. You can't just leave me like this."

There was something about the way he asked. It hit me in my soft spot. I knew I wouldn't be getting off the phone tonight without telling him at least a little of my lifelong struggle. So over the next hour, I revealed who I really was to him and what that all means. He really did not understand what the word transgender was. But I made sure I explained everything and answered all of his questions.

His feelings on the matter were mixed. Part of him completely understood because of who I was and represented during his younger years of life. But part of him was also sad and felt a sense of loss.

"I have to be honest with you, Dad, this isn't really a huge surprise for me. I mean you've obviously always been Dad, but something about you was different; softer. You just weren't like the other dads. I'm not saying this in a bad way, I'm just saying you were a dad that was also a bonus mom to me," he noted, then continued, "You were softer and emotional. Not that all moms are soft and emotional. There was always something about you I sensed, but I'm having a hard time putting my finger on what exactly *it* was. I just don't want to lose you. I don't want my dad to go away. I love you so much."

"Honey, I'm not going anywhere. I'm still here. I'm still the same person I've always been. The only difference, for now, is you know something about me now that you've never known. While it's true, there will be some physical changes you will notice, I will always be me. Who I am will never change, except my overall happiness for becoming congruent and a better version of myself."

This conversation was emotionally complex for me because I still recalled a few years back when Corey was about sixteen and dropped off the planet. He stopped taking my calls and never responded to my text messages. God knows I called him every single day and never gave up. Then, one day, he answered.

I immediately became choked up and asked, "Where have you been all this time, Corey? Why have you been non-responsive?"

After a momentary pause, Corey, with a voice of disdain asked, "How come you never paid Mom any child support?"

"What on Earth are you talking about? Where would you ever get such an idea that I didn't pay child support?"

"Mom told me. After you moved to Florida, she told me you were a deadbeat and didn't give her money. She said you were self-absorbed."

"Why didn't you come to me with this information before Corey? I'm so disappointed that you didn't at least attempt to ask me this question before you removed yourself from my life. So before you go any further, let me tell you that since day one, I paid your mom child support, and I paid your health insurance for most of your life. I have been paying for a life insurance policy with you as the sole beneficiary since the day you were born," I exclaimed.

I let him take that in, then continued, "I have every single receipt from the New York State Child Support Collection Unit and cashed check stubs from your mom from the past eighteen years. I also have my old insurance policies that show that you were a part of my family health plan."

"What are you trying to tell me? You mean she just made this stuff up?"

"Well, that's what it sure sounds like to me, Corey. I can't believe after all we've been through together that you would believe such an outrageous thing. We only get one life Corey and if you're willing to walk away from somebody, you'd better be crystal clear about why you're walking away. I'll be in New York to see Matthew and Tyler two weeks from now. You know, the trip I make from Florida to New York every five weeks on average that for the past year you suddenly became too busy to even be around your brothers? I suggest you show up this time. I will bring the receipts with me; not because I owe you anything, but to prove that you've been lied to on a level that I've never seen before."

"No, I believe you. I'm so sorry," he said with one of the saddest inflections I had heard from him.

"One of the most emotional things you ever told me was that your only fondest memories of childhood came from being with me and Christine. I never forgot that and never will," I said as I welled up again. "Whatever our relationship will be going forward, the one thing you're never allowed to do, is to break a promise. You can't make promises to Matthew and Tyler, then not come through on those promises like you've done many times this past year. Other than your love and trust, that's the one thing I want from you, Corey.

I never once broke a promise to you. Never. So don't do that to the boys, or someday, your own children."

"I'm sorry and I will definitely be there. I feel so bad right now."

"Well, don't feel bad. That's not the intention of my call. We're a family."

"I love you, Dad. I will stay in touch from now on. I promise."

∼

My family has had the honor of placing the Memorial Day flags at the gravesites of those that served our country since my dad was a child. We took care of several cemeteries in Monticello New York, about ten miles away from where I grew up in upstate New York. The only difference now was my dad, Papa and I now lived in Florida, which for obvious reasons made it logistically more difficult. But we maintained that our tradition and responsibility would not end simply because we lived far away.

That evening Corey and I finished our conversation in the parking lot of our hotel. It was far more emotional in person. A mixture of emotions had taken over him since we last talked about it. He couldn't shake the thought he could lose his dad.

"I know all of this is a lot for you to absorb. The last thing I ever wanted in your life was more complexity, thus one of the other reasons I never fully transitioned earlier. But there is one thing I want you to understand. I will always be your dad. I want you to remember that, Corey. There's one more thing I will tell only you."

"What's that?"

"When you were an infant right through into kindergarten, I spent just under $40,000 in attorney fees attempting to protect you and our relationship. I want you to know I would do the same thing all over again without any hesitation. But do you know what that money was really saved for?"

The Reveal

"A house, right?" he guessed.

"No. Something far more important for me. That money was to be used to transition when I was twenty-six years old, instead of now."

"Wait. You were going to transition back then?" he said in disbelief.

"Corey, I've been trying to transition since puberty. That $40,000 was going to help me transition and ensure our relationship stayed wonderful. By the time I was in my mid-twenties, I found a therapist just outside of New York City that helped others like me that had children. So, you were always priority number one since the day you were born."

"When are you going to tell Matthew and Tyler?" He asked.

"Soon enough. This doesn't exactly happen overnight, so I have time. But probably when they come down to me in two months. For now, let's focus on you and only you, okay? I really want you to be okay. Tomorrow at noon I scheduled our conference call with my therapist. She can answer questions you might have and help you understand the emotions you are feeling. It's your hour with her. Like I said before, you, and the other boys are the most important people in my life. So we're going to get this right the first go around, okay?"

July 2, 2018: Matthew, 13 and Tyler, 12

Driving to Orlando International Airport to meet my preteens, Matthew; thirteen, and Tyler; twelve, the worry about my impending conversation was building. I was questioning whether the conversations I had been having with myself for so many years would be good enough? But I shook these worries away, remembering that I have always excelled with impromptu speaking. "I got this," I affirmed. When I taught college courses, I could speak for an hour and a half from the top of my head, easily.

"Dad!" Tyler shouted and waved from down the long terminal walkway from the monorail. Matthew then waved as they drew closer. I was holding back a virtual flood of tears. The three of us embraced in a long hug, then headed to the car.

The initial plan was to do "the reveal" a few days after their arrival. But as we approached Tampa, I knew it would happen today.

"Tyler, can you call Mom and let her know we will be Skyping tonight at six."

"Why are we Skyping tonight?" Matthew asked.

"Well boys, I have something very important to tell you both. It's a very important conversation that I would like your mom to be a part of."

"Is something wrong?" Tyler asked rather concernedly.

"No, buddy. I'm fine. I just need to tell you guys something about me you don't know. And it's an important conversation we need to have together."

Six o'clock.

"Okay, guys—ready?" I asked.

With my tablet in hand and the screen facing the boys, I began the Skype call. Christine, a very organized person, answered straight away. "Hi, guys," she said with a hint of her laughter.

I had turned around the living room recliner and sat down while facing the boys on the couch before me. Their mom, full-screen on my Samsung.

"Boys, I have something important and rather different to tell you today. It is something Mom already knows," I began. "You know how the past year I have been talking about diversity?"

Tyler chimed in, "You mean about gay people and stuff?"

"Yes. Those conversations."

"Wow, Dad. You're gay?" Tyler asked with his usual sarcasm.

"Um. No. What I want to tell you boys is that for my entire life I haven't been strong enough to let you see the authentic person I am on the inside. I'm a unique person. When I was only four years old, I knew something was not correct with me. My brain told me I was a girl, but everyone else said I was a boy."

"Wait," Tyler once again jumped in. "So, you want to change into a girl, right?"

Before I could answer his question, their mom preempted me by responding, "Would you mind if I fielded this one?"

I was aghast. The most important question my son has ever asked me, and something I had been preparing to answer for his entire life was about to get answered instead by their mom?

"Um. Okay. No problem," I said anyway.

"Actually, Tyler, I've known about Dad for over twenty years now. And, no, your dad doesn't want to change into a girl. She already is. She just has boy parts. And now you guys know. And you know what, we're all going to be okay!"

I couldn't believe what I just heard and experienced. Their mom had just brilliantly articulated everything and more with the pure elegance of just a few brief sentences. I could never have answered Tyler's question with the pure elegance she had just displayed.

"How lucky am I to have just witnessed that from an ex?" I thought to myself.

Christine's words made me cry as soon as those amazing words left her lips. And as if on cue, she followed suit.

Witnessing the raw emotion of this made Tyler stand up and walk to me. He sat on my lap, then hugged me. "I love you so much. And you know what? See the way I'm hugging you right now? This is how I will always hug you forever and ever."

Christine and I were now engaged in full-on hyperventilation-style crying, which couldn't possibly get any worse when Tyler pulled out of the hug and executed a simple sign language phrase. He put his opened right hand up to his face with his thumb pointing at his chin and fingers pointing up. Then he rolled his fingers across the front of his face. Then immediately following, he closed his hand into a loose fist with his thumb pointing up toward his right ear and brought it down toward his chin. He had just literally signed "pretty girl."

What an amazing experience. I knew at that moment God blessed me. A few seconds later, and Matthew was hugging me. Instead of easing the boys into this, we continued the discussion and answered all of their questions. The conversation that at first was to be only twenty minutes, became a two-hour beautiful event.

"I kind of knew it would be something like this. You said you were getting earrings to get back into a band." Tyler laughed.

Matthew chimed in and said, "Yeah, it's not too hard to figure out where you were going with all of those conversations we had in New York when you would visit. I just never put it all together even though we talked about this stuff every five weeks."

"What do we call you now? Like should we stop calling you Dad? And are you changing your name? What's your girl name?" I replied, "The name I gave to myself at eight years old is Amber Rose Washington."

As I continued to let them in on where that name came from, I said, "I have no desire to have you call me anything but Dad. Mom is your mom—forever. And although I may eventually look and sound different, we should all recognize that I will always be the dad to four wonderful boys. A dad who also is a woman."

Matthew said he believed one kid in his class may be trans or perhaps non-binary. They knew things most adults don't understand. This is because we live in a society where the conversation has finally begun. Believe it or not, kids know who they are. Although there are many parents that insist their child is "confused", the reality is quite the opposite.

Later in the week, I took them to the Salvador Dali Museum in St. Petersburg. On the way home, an incredible thought came to me, so I vocalized it. I said, "Boys?"

"Yes?" they replied.

"Never could I have ever imagined in a million years asking my teenage boys, 'Hey guys. Mind if we go through puberty together?'"

The laughter filled the car with an abundance of positive energy.

"You know something? It's good to have a sense of humor; no matter what."

~

Sure. Everything's just peachy. I live a charmed life with coming out, right? Wrong. I had my share of hurtful responses that went from plain ignorance to the downright terrible. For the record, I've had successful and empathetic responses somewhere in the 90th percentile of the two hundred plus people I came out to. But there were a few people that did not respond as enthusiastically, or even at all. Honestly, many of the poo-pooers were equating my circumstance to sinful behavior and impure thoughts, selfishness, and hysterically; "a midlife crisis" because of my three divorces. And then there were a few who said, "I totally accept you, *but* . . . "

That's the thing, you know? The vast majority of us that are trans end up dealing with the loss of family and friends. For many of us, the loss is disastrous and the toll enormous. For others, like myself, the loss hurt, but it was manageable. Although I had a sliver of adversity within my family with a few aunts, uncles, and cousins, I'm not losing any sleep over any of it. This is not to say, that some of them really hurt me.

"You want to have an *exorcism* performed on me? Really?"

It was surreal. Was I actually being cast for the remake of the movie, *The Exorcist*?

"Just repeat the prayer of Saint Benedict over and over and he'll remove any demonic forces currently making you fall away from Christ," they'd say.

Hiding From Myself

To this day, I love this close relative more than they know, but I can't help but feel sorry for them. They have dedicated their entire life to foolish, ill-conceived, man-made religious mythology. I guess you can say, to them, I became *the leper* of the family.

My curiosity was piqued. I needed to understand why so many family members and friends become so distant or outright hostile towards us when they learn we are trans? And how does that rejection, stigma, and too often; violence, affect us as trans women?

A long history of gender stereotyping, predominantly governed by a male-oriented patriarchal society, is surely at the center of the issue. However, going past that obvious factor, when the *DSM-III* added "gender identity disorder" as a mental disorder in 1980, it contributed to an increase in stigmatization, especially among transgender women.

When we first attempt to reveal our authentic selves to our core family, far too often it leads to rejection or violence. These hostile negative acts leave us more vulnerable to poor self-image, unhealthy behaviors, poor health, and suicide. Is it any wonder that so many trans women end up on the streets littered with challenges, not only of navigating the loss of their family, but also their quality of life—food, shelter, employment, personal safety, and no health care? Is it any wonder that these same individuals end up with an increased prevalence of HIV and other sexually transmitted diseases? And is it any wonder that drug and alcohol abuse, violence, incarceration, and suicide are all too commonplace within our demographic?

Think it through. Society typically looks down upon the very demographic I just described. They mock and spit in the face of "their lifestyle" and believe that those negative outcomes are the status quo. However, society created this demographic, not the other way around. Ideologies based on rigid and limiting definitions of gender and sexuality are to blame for many of the negative outcomes in the lives of transgender individuals.

The Reveal

Even today, parents that understand diversity become the victims of ridicule and discrimination when allowing their child to be who they are. Those that ridicule often say, "How dare you allow your son to behave like a girl! That's child abuse!"

But society and its people can be troublesome when it comes to unlearning old untruths and replacing them with logical and objective meanings. Humans do not fare well in this unlearning process. The current average for unlearning old untruths; that is things thought to be fact, but were outright incorrect, is about two to three hundred years. Yes, I wrote that correctly.

Look back at society's ridiculous religious ideology that described leprosy. They considered those that suffered the disease socially unacceptable; unclean. This unfortunate stigmatism would last from the days before Jesus until the mid-twentieth century.

> I often call myself, a testosterone survivor.

Okay, so why mention leprosy twice in this book? People are pre-wired to judge a book by its cover. It takes genuine effort to change that programming. The same applies for profiling trans women. If you had to go through puberty the wrong way the first time around, like me, the result is massive and permanent testosterone damage. In fact, I often call myself, "a testosterone survivor." Testosterone severely fucks with your height, muscular features, body contouring, facial features, facial and body hair, loss of hair on the scalp, deepening voice, etc. These traits all give others an unconscious profile of your sex/gender within just a few milliseconds.

Many of us endure countless hours of painful procedures to repair the damage done by our first puberty. There's laser hair removal, electrolysis, facial feminization surgeries, tracheal shaves, vaginoplasty, bilateral orchiectomy, breast augmentation, and, of course, hormone replacement therapy (HRT). We endure all of this pain, and the pain is like nothing I've ever known, so we can experience life closer to what everyone else takes for granted.

> After our disastrous puberty; if we make it through in the first place, we live our lives attempting to assimilate and conform to what society expects us to be.

Many generations of trans women grew up as trans girls, usually hidden. Each of us struggling each day with incongruity. We suffer from being perceived differently by our peers—even when we are not yet out. This typically results in jeering, bullying, and physical assaults. So for most of us, we remember our childhoods ranging from bittersweet memories to downright awful. Many of today's trans girls are still forced to endure puberty the wrong way. Ninety-nine percent of you don't have the foggiest idea how tragic that is because you lack a basic framework to understand, and that's not entirely your fault. After our disastrous puberty; if we make it through in the first place, we live our lives attempting to assimilate and conform to what society expects us to be, or we take the leap of faith and transition, leading to a whole new world of scrutiny; just to be who we are and live authentically.

I speak for myself when I say this. There are very few upsides to being trans. It's not fun. I never wanted this and hope the new generations can stave off that first puberty, by delaying it (with puberty blockers), then proceeding with the correct puberty when they are ready. It will surely make their quality of life exponentially greater. If there is one thing I have learned about myself along this complicated rebirth into womanhood, it is that I am unique. I have a unique perspective on humanity. I am far more empathetic than most because I don't like to see others struggling silence as I did. I pay attention to details in people that most miss in a lifetime. I am very "person-centered."

I am unafraid and unapologetic when I state that my philosophy contradicts the conservative mindset. Far too many people still judge

The Reveal

a book by its cover and believe they are better than other types of people. Far too many people hold on to mythology and old, incorrect information. I, just like so many others am but one illness away from being that emaciated homeless person you see walking around town. I have little to give, but you can count on me doing something good for somebody every chance I get. You don't know each person's story. You assume it. What a shame. We label these people as "leeches", "lazy", "mental." It's tragic.

The same delivery system is at play when it comes to people like me. But I stand proud of who I am. I stand firm in the face of adversity. When someone stares at me with that look of disgust, I look them straight in the eyes, smile, pick up my right hand, and give a little friendly wave, and politely say, "Hi." Regardless of your stares, I am me. This is me. Accept me or don't accept me, it doesn't change who I am or who I've always been.

> I was fruitlessly searching for love externally without first understanding the wonder of myself.

The coming out experience has transformed me from an insecure and fearful person into a confident, independent, and caring woman who loves and adores herself. It has awakened my spirit by allowing me to release my eyes from seeing and my ego from defending. It has also made me realize I was fruitlessly searching for love externally without first understanding the wonder of myself.

Yes. I had learned valuable lessons that helped me become the person I am. But I was about to be side-swiped with a whole new level of adversity and struggle.

Stalled in Transition

January 3, 2019

Nearly an hour had already passed within the blink of an eye. There I was lying on the unbearably cold hard platform just after my CT scan. I was visibly shaking, not just because it felt as cold as an Alaskan winter within the room, but because I was most likely in shock. A nurse, doctor, or lab tech; at the time I just couldn't tell the difference, said, "You have what appears to be a small occlusion in the right hemisphere of your brain. Although we will need to perform further tests, it appears you are having an ischemic stroke. We need to administer a drug called TPA. It's a strong clot dissolving medicine; a clot buster. It's very important that we disclose to you that there is a risk of death that comes with the administration of this drug. Do you understand? Do we have your consent to administer this drug?"

Those words terrified me. I had a million thoughts, each one demanding my full attention, all at the same time. Would these be my final few moments of life? I don't want to die and leave my kids! I finally began my metamorphosis to becoming the person I was always meant to be, and now that has all disappeared within the past hour. Although my mind was playing out all the worst-case scenarios in unison, I was able to answer her question without a second thought. "Please, yes. Whatever you need to do. Yes, you have my permission."

Before proceeding, she asked, "Did you take any medication before or during your current symptoms?"

"Yes. I've always carried a 325 mg aspirin with me. When I realized I was having stroke symptoms, I quickly placed it under my tongue and let it dissolve sublingually."

She looked at me with both admiration and concern, "That was a very risky move, because if this had been a hemorrhagic stroke, that decision could have been fatal."

As she administered the TPA, she motioned for the tech to place another warm blanket on my shaking body.

Within moments, I was already on my way to the ICU where I would spend the next three days. During the ten-minute trip to the ICU, I began recalling every moment and detail leading up to my current circumstance.

～

Working in the Westshore district of Tampa was exciting and beautiful. Our building complex was about a block from the bay itself. The only obstacle between our building and the bay was the FBI complex, with which we shared a common easement. The biggest drawback was getting to and from work. Rush hour in Tampa is impossible, especially along the I-275 corridor. There's just no convenient way to get anywhere, let alone home during rush hour, which typically ran from 3:45 p.m. until nearly seven o'clock. I would typically leave the office around six and regularly expected to spend close to the next hour in stop-and-go traffic on my twelve mile journey home.

After an uneventful day, I said goodnight to the remaining three people in the office before exiting the building and making my way to my car. Just like any other day, I got into my car, fixed my hair in the rearview mirror, strapped in, and slowly backed the car out of a random parking space in our rather large corporate parking lot. As I made my way towards the road, I suddenly felt a strange electrical charge on the left side of my body. The electrical charge started in my left hand and fingers but then quickly traveled the entire length of my left arm. Within just another second or two, the electrical charge had engulfed the entirety of the left side of my body.

As I continued to pull out of the parking lot, my left hand fell off the steering wheel onto my lap. I could no longer move nor feel my left arm. Literally everything on the left side of my body was going numb, which now also included the left side of my face. I knew at that very instant I was having a stroke. I used my right hand to turn back into the parking lot and pulled up to the front entrance of the building. I was simultaneously voice-calling one of my coworkers, Anthony, whom I had just left.

"Anthony. I'm parked at the front entrance of the building and I'm having a stroke. I need your help!" I was quickly becoming hysterical, so he knew I was serious, "Please help me. Please help me!" I pleaded with panicked breath.

Apparently upon hearing the word stroke, Anthony was already flying down the stairs from our second-floor suite. Within seconds he was racing towards my car. As he approached, I opened my door with my right hand.

"What can I do? What can I do?"

As difficult as it was, I tried to stay as calm as I could. I knew that we had to get to the hospital and fast. I told him, "I need you to drive me to the hospital while I call 911."

He helped me walk to the passenger side of my car and got me situated inside the car, as he prepared to get me to the hospital posthaste. As he drove, my symptoms worsened. I had Anthony dial 911 for me. I informed the dispatcher I was having a stroke and my friend had me en route to St Joseph's hospital. The dispatcher connected me with an emergency responder who asked how far out we were from the hospital. Considering our current distance, just under four miles, and the sheer number of cars jammed up between us and the hospital, the emergency responder instructed that Anthony continue towards the hospital as we would beat the ambulance. He also reminded Anthony to continue to abide by all traffic safety laws.

"We will inform the hospital that you are en route and describe your symptoms so the rapid response team can be ready to meet you."

After hanging up, all I could think about were my four boys, my dad, and my sister.

After briefly calling my dad, I was already calling my five-year-old's mother and told her of my current situation. Ensuring I didn't frighten him, I began, "Hi Jack. I hope you're having a nice day. I miss you. I have to go take care of something right now and might not call you later like I usually do, okay? But when I'm all done, I will, okay? I love you so much! Can you give me a big kiss over the phone?"

Just like he always did when I asked that question, he greeted the microphone of his mom's phone with a huge lip smack, "Mwah!"

I gave him a huge kiss right back and said, "I'm hugging you right now, okay. I love you so much, Jack."

"I love you so much, Daddy."

I had him hand his mom the phone and told her that somebody would be in touch with her to let her know how I am doing.

Traffic was unbearable. I felt it was taking far too long to get to the hospital. We had been on the road for over ten minutes and we were only halfway there. I began to panic, which I am sure did not help my situation as my symptoms deepened yet again. Now the entire left side of my face was almost completely numb, I had the worst headache of my life, and I was finding it harder and harder to speak. I was starting to slur my words. I still had to call my three other boys, and I didn't know if I'd even be able to speak.

Nothing else in the world mattered. If I was on my way out, I would ensure I told each one of my children how much I loved them at least one more time!

Not sounding like myself anymore, I articulated, "Hi Christine. Sorry to bother you, but I am on my way to the hospital. I'm having a stroke. If they are there, can I just quickly tell the boys I love them?"

She immediately gave one of the boys the phone.

Hi Dad. What's up? Tyler asked.

"Tyler, can you please put me on speakerphone so Matthew can hear me? This is very, very important."

I knew he could hear the horror in my voice, not to mention I was already slurring my words.

"Boys, I'm on my way to the hospital. I don't want you to worry about me, but I wanted to call you both and tell you how much I love you, okay?"

"What's wrong? Tell me? What is happening? And what's wrong with your voice?" they both asked with obvious anxious concern.

"I am most likely having a stroke. I am hoping Mom can tell you what that means."

The boys didn't even know what to say. I knew they were in shock. And that made me cry. Even though they were both teenagers, I wondered at that moment if I should have even told them that amount of detail. But I needed to tell them how much I loved them, even more so because I was only seeing them every five weeks.

"Boys, I will have Papa or somebody call you and let you know how I'm doing a little later okay. I just wanted to call you and give you the biggest kiss over the phone I can. I love you boys so much," I repeated.

We were about one thousand feet from the hospital entrance and stuck at the longest red light in human history. It had taken us nearly twenty minutes to travel a little less than four miles. I had just one more call to make, my eldest son, Corey. I already knew I would not be able to get a hold of him. He, at twenty-three years old, was harder to reach than the President. So I voice texted him to let him know what was going on.

Other than the enormous empathetic sense of loss I felt within all the hearts of my children if I were not to make it, probably the biggest disappointment cycling through my head since the symptoms began was that my transition was over. "I'm not going to be congruent like I've always wanted to be." I repeated to myself. At that very moment it felt that no matter what happened, I had been handed a death sentence.

Upon arriving at the hospital, the rapid response team was already waiting for me. They placed me in a wheelchair and took me to a triage room, where they asked me several questions that I could barely answer audibly. They immediately moved me to a stretcher and started making their way down the hallway. As they approached the attending ER physician, they stopped the stretcher, as a nurse poked and prodded my right arm to get an IV started.

Although there were bigger things to worry about at the moment, I was nervous because I was inside of a Catholic hospital. I had absolutely no idea how they would respond to somebody like me. Somebody that's transgender.

The attending physician came up to me and said, "How long have you been having symptoms?"

I let him know my best guess, which at the time was about forty minutes. He then asked me if I was taking any medication.

I told him straight out of the gate I was transgender. "I take 100mg of spironolactone and 4mg of estradiol daily."

"I understand. So you are transitioning from female to male?"

Here I was in the middle of a stroke, thinking *this is the end of my life* and the only thought occupying my head at that exact moment was, "Fuck My Life! He just got my transition completely backwards."

"No. I just started my transition. I am the opposite. They assigned me male at birth."

He was a very kind man and said, "I'm very sorry for the mistake." He then informed the nurses and other people attending to me I was transgender. When he referred to me, he used the correct pronouns; she and her. That small gesture of affirmation made me feel just a little better through the shit show I was experiencing.

After completely ruining my right arm trying to start an IV, they placed me into another triage room. They began hooking me up to all sorts of monitoring equipment while they waited for the next available slot to get me a CT scan. The attending nurse was a guy in his late twenties who neither had nor passed a class in diversity training.

The attending physician gave the nurse a rundown of what I was experiencing, told him I was transgender, and referred to me as she and her. However, when the physician left, this nurse took the opportunity to misgender me every chance he got. This was not a case of someone making an honest mistake. This was belligerent.

"Okay, SIR. I need you to lift your right leg up in the air and try to hold it there, okay, SIR!"

"And now I need you to lift up your left leg, SIR!"

"SIR, my name is Jason. I'll be watching you until they move you to your room. Okay, DUDE!"

Stroke or no stroke, I had had enough of his blatantly biased, obnoxious, rude attitude.

I retaliated, but with a sense of very firm pragmatism. "Listen. I'm having a stroke. Is it remotely possible for you to be less of an asshole to me right now? There's no reason for you to be repeatedly misgendering me."

I don't really know how this person became a nurse because his intelligence and empathy level were not up to par for the position that he held. He said, rather sarcastically, "First of all, I know what you are. And I am a nurse, not your psychotherapist. And, yes, you are a sir."

"I heard the attending physician make it extremely clear to you that I'm transgender and obviously you have an issue with that. Unless you want me to speak to someone of much higher authority than your pay grade allows, I suggest you stop. Jesus. I can't believe this."

He walked out of the room and started talking to someone in the hallway just outside my door. I could hear him saying, "The guy in this room is the *stroke alert*, and he thinks he's a woman. Total mental case."

That was all I needed. I'm having a stroke and someone is treating me subhuman; not to mention, completely ignoring the Nurse's Pledge. In part, it states, " . . . I promise to respect at all times the dignity of the patient in my charge . . . "

Another nurse entered the room and asked how I was feeling. "I don't feel any worse, but I do feel extremely tired and . . . " I paused. "We have another problem."

"What can I help you with ma'am?" she politely responded.

"First, thank you for not misgendering me. Second, I don't want that other person, Jason, in this room again. He has been purposely misgendering me repeatedly and being viciously biased. And he just called me a mental case to one of his coworkers. I'm so sorry, but it's making me exponentially more stressed out than I already am."

"Don't you be sorry. That kind of behavior is unacceptable. You take a deep breath for me and relax. I will take care of this immediately. She walked outside of my room and spoke with two individuals, one of which was Jason. During her questioning of nurse Jason, he denied saying anything of the sort.

"I didn't say any of that. That guy is making this up."

She immediately keyed into his obvious use of the word, "that guy", and then the other person excused him for the entire evening and told him his shift was over and to go home.

She walked back in and said, "I'm so sorry about that. Don't you worry. I have another nurse on her way right now. I know you are going through a lot, so let's focus on getting you better. I apologize for his behavior. It was unprofessional, and worse, lacking basic human compassion."

∽

The first night in ICU was unnerving. I kept saying to myself, "I'm in the Intensive Care Unit. Oh, my God, am I going to make it?"

Whatever they had administered to me or maybe it was just the stroke itself had me extremely tired. If it weren't for the doctors and nurses continually coming into the room taking vital signs, asking questions, and taking blood, I would have probably had a restful sleep.

I had nine nurses, and CNAs that worked with me over the next three days. Each one of them seemed genuinely interested in my life story. They would ask questions about my situation and life and I would elaborate. The chatterbox I am seemed to pique their interest.

They were back into my room as often as they could get there to hear a little more about my life as a transgender person in hiding, while meeting and working with celebrities in the music business.

> When other women speak to you as they do other women, that is affirmation—and that, my friends, is what it is all about.

Each nurse became a friend to me. Although my transition had only just begun, they knew quite distinctly that they were not having conversations with a guy. They understood that I was really no different from any of them. When you are someone like me it's a wonderful thing to behold when other women speak to you as they do other women. That—is affirmation, and that, my friends, is what it is all about.

I was so happy to have just a few visitors while I was there. My friend Anthony saved my life. He and his wife Leslie stayed in my room that first night as long as the ICU permitted them. It really fills a person's heart to have such beautiful friends that care. My dad would arrive the next day along with my favorite person, Debbie (whom I still call my twin flame), who had to make a cameo with presents in-hand.

The following afternoon they had me scheduled for an MRI to see the extent of the damage the stroke may have caused. I was already feeling much better. I had regained feeling and use of the left side of my body except for weird intermittent numbness that would sweep through my arm to my fingertips and occasionally on the left side of my head.

Later that evening, the neurologist confirmed that I had an ischemic stroke, but luckily the damage was not very extensive and fully recoverable. He said you are a very lucky person. That 325 mg aspirin you took, along with the TPA that we administered, saved your life and put you inside of what we call the 12 percent club. Those are the stroke survivors that are likely to make a full recovery. I was so relieved that I cried.

On the third day in ICU they told me they would release me from the hospital. They said it's unorthodox because usually people from the ICU typically end up going to a regular hospital bed for a few days before being discharged. But because of my unusually fast recovery, they were discharging me directly from the ICU.

Some nurses gave me their email addresses and told me to stay in touch. That was exactly the affirmation that I needed from these wonderful women. The little things in life I always desired were things like this. Being friends with other women, that know I am just another woman. Each of them thanked me for our conversations. They said they learned so much about something that they had never really come in close contact with before, other than in their coursework.

Over the next month I would be on a cocktail of anticoagulants and other medications that would hopefully stave off a second stroke.

While at my cardiology follow-up appointment I asked the specialist, "What do I do about my transition? I was scheduled to have my confirmation surgery in August on my birthday."

With the emotion of a pet rock, he said, "You can't have any surgeries. You just had a stroke. You will be on blood thinners for the rest of your life, so you need to get that idea out of your head. If you want to live, you're done with that lifestyle."

I couldn't believe my ears. Here was another person with absolutely no idea what being transgender was. He had no sense of compassion or empathy. With his nurse standing right behind him, I looked him straight in the eyes and I said, "First, being transgender is *not* a lifestyle. You're a doctor. Why would you even say something so offensive? I'm not a cardiologist, so I can't argue with your medical assessment, but I can argue that you are very insensitive and offensive. So, from this moment forward, you are no longer my cardiologist."

With the bold confidence that allowed me to speak my mind to him, I stood up, politely said goodbye to the nurse, and left the office. I immediately called Debbie and told her what had just happened. She was livid. She was very proud of my response and said she would get me a real cardiologist and team to work with. Within a day she had given me the name of one of the best electrophysiologists in Tampa, Dr. James Irwin. She said there were also cardiologists within that practice that would be very caring and professional to me.

Within only a week, I had already made an appointment. I asked one receptionist if they might call me into the office using my preferred name that was not yet legal. Although their computer system had no option for this, she took care of it and said it would not be a problem.

I had amassed an impressive amount of confidence over the past few months. I used to be insecure and hyperaware of people looking at me, but now, I was just confident. I knew the process I was going through would take years, but that no longer meant hiding who I was. I am a woman and I carry myself quite well, thank you very much. I walked into the enormous waiting room with seating for at least forty or fifty people. It was also apparently a busy day, because there weren't many seats left. Although much more confident, I still took that extra second to take a deep breath as I entered the room, before making my way to the large reception counter on the opposite side of the room.

During my appointment, I told Dr. Irwin what my ex-cardiologist had told me about never being able to transition. His face turned to that of befuddlement as he said, "That's not true. There are other ways we can handle this so you can continue your transition." I immediately knew this was the doctor for me.

Over the next six months I would go through countless cardiac tests and three reparative heart procedures. The first was cardiac ablation to help prevent further bouts of atrial fibrillation. The second was the installation of a device called *The Watchman* that, when installed, completely seals off my left atrial appendage, thus preventing blood clots from exiting my heart. The third, performed on the same day as my second procedure, was the installation of an occluder, a device that plugs up holes they found in my heart.

The occluder was a device of particular importance as they learned I had a congenital heart defect. Apparently I had been born with two holes in my heart. They now had the most likely reason I had an ischemic stroke.

I was so tired all the time. I was still having PVCs (premature ventricular contractions) every day, all day long. The surgeon, Dr. Irwin had attempted to ablate them, but apparently while they sedated me, my PVCs would subside making it nearly impossible for him to ablate them.

Somehow—I made it. I made it through the most difficult year of my life. I recovered from my stroke within days. I weathered three heart procedures. I'm finally within reach of what they consider a full recovery.

Admittedly, I was in a serious clinical depression for nearly the entire year of 2019. I was also anxiety-stricken each time any feeling within my body that reminded me of the first stroke occurred. Not only did I have to make a remarkable physical recovery, but I also had to make the same recovery from the anxiety to move forward successfully.

It's a new year. 2020 has begun. It's time to reboot my life and get back on track with a fresh sense of optimism. I made an appointment with my cardiologist, Dr. Sai. I told him of my intentions to begin the forward movement once again with my transition, specifically my surgeries; with his medical blessing, so to speak.

Dr. Sai is one of those cardiologists that is genuine. Not only did he handle my medical condition brilliantly, but his authentic and genuine interest in me successfully saw me continue to work through my transition that awkwardly had been in a full stop for the past year.

"I have a plan Dr. Sai," I stated rather confidently. "I want to continue my electrolysis especially in my genital area so I can, at least by the summer, have my gender confirmation surgery (GCS), which includes my vaginoplasty. So I will need a letter of consent from you clearing the way with my surgeon in Pennsylvania to perform the surgery and to deal with my medical insurance."

Dr. Sai, tuned in to what I was saying and fully understanding my medical condition, healing process, and goals said, "Amber. I would be most happy to get that letter written for you straightaway. We will send it to you as soon as we can so you can provide it to your insurance and surgeon. I'm very excited for you. In fact, we are all excited for you," he said, as he turned towards his nurse, who also stated her support. "You've been through a lot, and you deserve to be happy, Amber."

I was beyond ecstatic. Within twenty-four hours I had my confirmation letter in hand. I immediately called Dr. McGinn's office in Pennsylvania and told them I received my confirmation, which cleared me for surgery. I called my insurance company and set up the required pre-authorization. I made an appointment immediately to see her recommended electrologist in Pennsylvania so she could quickly finish that horrid process before my vaginoplasty. Everything was lining up perfectly and quickly! I was finally back into living life, right?

Holy Legal Red Tape Batman

After such a tragic year, the last thing I needed was to deal with more shit. But as it would be, "shit happens." Apparently the anesthesia caused a condition called telogen effluvium. This is a condition in which your hair falls out after a stressful experience. It had been six months since the last heart surgery. I saw a dermatologist who told me that typically six months after a very stressful experience and/or from anesthesia, the stress pushes large numbers of hair follicles into the resting phase. The dermatologist said I could expect to lose about 50 percent of my hair.

My hair was falling out in a massive way and at times coming out in heaping clumps.

Once again I looked up and shouted at God, "Seriously! I've come so far. I have overcome some tragic shit God, and now I'm going to lose my hair; a woman's crown jewel. Couldn't you let me enjoy my longer hair for a little while first?"

But there was nothing I could do. What was going to happen was going to happen. So I decided to press on. There is so much to do, and I'm not about to give up now. It was time to tackle the legal complexities.

Many women understand the complexities and bureaucracies built into changing their name. But many people don't understand the complexities and bureaucracies they have built into changing your name when you are an individual that is transgender. There's a lot more red tape.

Before we dive into the legalities of name changes and gender marker changes, we have to tackle something else first.

Being transgender has become politicized. That's like politicizing somebody that has leukemia, or cleft palate, or autism. No society, especially ours, should be politicizing variations of the diverse human condition.

> We don't choose to be who we are, we just are who we are—just like you are who you are.

Many people believe that if you're transgender, you're part of an ideology. It's not an ideology. I sure as hell didn't learn to be transgender. I didn't sign up to be in some club or join some whacko cult. Ideologies are things people teach us. You can't teach somebody to be transgender. You either are or you are not. End of discussion. Game over. We don't *choose* to be who we are, we just are who we are—just like you are who you are.

We also must tackle some blatantly politicized rhetoric and mythology from other members of a toxic administration that began in 2017. These people and, one person in particular, who I shall not name, said in one of his presidential addresses, not only do transgender people not belong in the military but their surgeries cost taxpayers hundreds of thousands of dollars each, not to mention they take massive amounts of drugs. Do you want to pay your hard-earned tax dollars for their surgeries?

Okay, so now let's shovel away all the bullshit and get down to brass tacks and reality.

First, let's cover GCS, which is an acronym for gender confirmation surgery. Gender confirmation surgery is actually a procedure called vaginoplasty in my case. I had scheduled it not once, but twice. The first cancellation was because of my stroke, and the second because of the COVID-19 pandemic.

This incredibly life-altering and important procedure does not cost over $250,000 dollars as the current president so deceptively stated, okay. I am having my surgery performed by one of the best surgeons in the country and it's being done for less than $24,000 for someone without insurance coverage. And since the entire medical community understands that this is a medical condition, most insurance plans cover the surgery for the same cost.

To help someone become congruent is saving their life. If you're outside of the realm of understanding that crucial point, you are probably scratching your head in bewilderment. But it's true. So, we have the president claiming it costs several hundred thousand dollars and someone that's about to have it done saying that it will cost about $24,000. Also, keep in mind the medical establishment can easily give anyone confirmation of these facts. All Donnie can give you are his insane, uneducated tweets. Please, I am not making cheap shots at our president. He did that all by himself. As far as taking massive amounts of drugs? Is he serious? Where does he even dig this shit up?

First, we do not take massive amounts of drugs. Not trans men nor trans women. There is the Harry Benjamin Standards of Care and WPATH that provide the safety guidelines physicians follow when treating trans people. They want the hormones administered to us at the lowest dosage to achieve success. Massive amounts of drugs? Wow.

Then there is the argument, it's too much cost to bear. It will cost us between $2.4 million and $8.4 million annually—let's pretend those numbers are magically accurate. If we compare the total Defense Department spending on erectile dysfunction medications, such as Viagra, well that alone exceeds $80 million each year. So, "We here in the American military, we promote and advocate for massive Hard-Ons for our troops!" Give me a break!

Another mythological campaign that exists is that transgender people are perverts that want to go into women's bathrooms to peek at other women. People who believe this are so blindly lost in the vitriol and rhetoric of this misinformation hate campaign, they can't and won't see the truth. The reality is I'm a woman and my brain is wired exactly like every other woman's brain. Bathrooms are gross. I want to stand in the shortest line so I can pee, wash my hands, fix my makeup and hair, and move on with my fucking life. Yet somehow in some alternative ass-backward, backwoods universe, they label people like me perverts! Listen closely, the only people that are perverts are the people accusing us of being perverts in the first place! There have been scores of incidents and arrests of disgusting, ignorant people peeking under *our* bathroom stalls to see if we have a penis. I mean seriously, what the hell is the fascination with our genitals? That only proves that those fixated on our genitals are the perverts. Okay. Let's dive back into the legal stuff: changing your name and gender marker.

Changing your name legally along with your gender marker can be stressful and draining. There are a lot of things that need to happen behind the scenes. Contrary to the belief of some individuals, it is not as easy as telling the DMV or other agency that you're a woman and voilà you're now a woman; easy peasy. That's not how this works. That's not how any of this works.

Depending on your state, you need a working history with a qualified therapist. This therapist would have to have given you a diagnosis that shows you have a history of incongruity and that you are a female, as in my case. I have several decades of documentation. I didn't need it. But I needed my therapist to write a letter affirming that I am, without question, female.

Second, you need to have your doctor and/or endocrinologist write a letter they sign before a notary. This letter confirms the diagnosis

Post-Reveal Adventures

It would be an amazing day. My teenage boys Matthew and Tyler were to arrive at Orlando International Airport At 12:30 p.m. Since the airport was a little over an hour away, I wanted to ensure I would get to the airport in plenty of time before their arrival. I had my best friend Moriah and my son Jack with me so all of us could spend the day in Orlando. Jack was so excited that he would soon be with his big brothers. It wasn't often that he could see them, since we live so far away. And since my stroke, I could not fly up every four to five weeks like I used to.

We arrived at the airport about thirty minutes early. We found perfect seating in the enormous main terminal lobby, directly facing the monorail walkway they would be using. It was a busy day at the terminal with people racing to get in the lengthy security line. Sitting next to us was a young mom with her little baby. The baby was definitely newborn and was comfortably nestled inside her carrier. Her mom had an anxious look on her face. This made me curious, and I'm chatty as hell. So, as they say, when in Rome . . .

I leaned over and said, "Your baby is so adorable."

"Thank you. We're waiting for my husband to get back. He's in the military. He deployed to Afghanistan several months ago, so he has not seen his new baby girl yet."

"Oh, my God. Really?" I replied. And without hesitation, I asked her if anyone was going to record a video of this incredible moment. I mean, this was like one of those tearjerker 20/20 storyline moments.

She said, "Unfortunately no, it's just me."

"If you'd like me to, I can record the entire event with your smartphone? This is far too special a moment to not capture."

This brought tears to her eyes as she barely could form the words, "Thank you so much! That's so thoughtful of you."

I said, "I just think this is an amazing moment that someday you can show your daughter. It will be a precious keepsake and moment for the rest of your lives. Trust me, I have four boys."

Within only a few minutes she could see him in the distance walking towards the terminal. She stood up with nervous excitement and handed me her phone.

Then, there he was. Her handsome husband, in uniform, returning home from what would hopefully be his final tour of duty. She started crying immediately as they embraced each other. Within that same instant she picked up their newborn baby girl as he held out his arms to receive her for the very first time.

The sight of this moment had me swelling with emotion and tears. Who wouldn't be, right? But I needed to focus on regaining my composure. The last thing this beautiful family needed in their keepsake was an overly emotional woman crying in the background during their moment.

I walked around them several times attempting to get the best shot possible. I continued recording for nearly five minutes. During my infringement of this private moment, he looked at his wife and asked who I was.

She said, "Her name is Amber. I met her just a few minutes ago, and she was so kind to offer to record this special memory for us."

He looked at me with his own tears welling up in his eyes and said, "Thank you so much, ma'am. You're very kind. I appreciate you doing this for us."

Well, that simple thank you was all I needed to start the waterworks flowing. So I figured it was time to stop recording, give back her phone, and let them enjoy whatever privacy they had in the busy terminal.

My boys hadn't even arrived yet, and I already had a doozy of an emotional day. I was definitely well-primed for the emotional greeting we would have in just a matter of minutes.

Jack was the first to see them walking towards the terminal, just like the soldier and new daddy had moments before. Jack began jumping up and down. "They're here. They're here, Daddy!"

I started recording with my smartphone if only to capture little Jack running up to his big brothers after not seeing them for nearly six months. This was important not just for me, but more so for Jack.

After hugging Jack, they immediately made their way to me. I stopped recording and hugged them for what seemed to be an eternity. Matthew and Tyler had grown at least three inches each and were now taller than me. I had not been in the physical presence of my boys in nearly half a year. It had been emotionally unbearable, so this would become the world's longest hug—like Guinness Book-worthy.

After greeting Moriah, to whom they were already very familiar, we made our way back to the parking garage and headed towards Disney Springs, Walt Disney World's remodeled, enormous shopping, dining and entertainment complex. Actually, the words enormous can't describe how large this part of Disney has become over the past few years.

We decided we would spend the afternoon exploring the newly designed complex and have a little fun while we were at it. There were plenty of themed restaurants that we could choose from, lots of stores that everyone in our group would find entertaining, and a very large movie complex where we would watch the newest *Lion King* movie later in the day.

The summer heat in Florida is always—well; hot. But today is just stupid hot! Beyond hot! Like, what were we thinking, hot! Within minutes of walking down the main thoroughfare by the lake, we already needed to stop and get everybody some water. And an hour later we had each consumed two bottles of water, except for Jack who was still working on his second.

Moriah and I led the group to one of the nearby restroom areas. The boys didn't seem to need to use the facilities, so we found them some shade right outside the door while Moriah and I made our way to the ladies' room and waited in the stereotypically long line. Somehow that simple visit to the ladies' room made us feel as if we had just trekked the impossible line to *Tower of Terror*.

"There are so many shops," Tyler said.

Everything from the Lego store to the Marvel Superhero Headquarters store, there was no shortage of places, over 150 to be more precise, we could duck into, to catch a break from the heat. We did more window shopping and got some snacks before getting the tickets for the movie. We walked around, stopping in a lot of very nice stores and candy shops for another two hours, again drinking lots of water. This time everyone was ready to use the restrooms. So we found yet another nearby restroom facility. This time Moriah and I would wait for the boys to take Jack into the men's room, and upon their return, we would make our way into the ladies' room line.

After washing my hands, fixing my makeup, which had melted off my face, and touching up my hair, Moriah and I made our way back out of the restroom. Nearly to the door, a pretentious thirty-something-year-old woman looked me straight in the eyes and shouted, "Oh my God! Like, totally wrong restroom!"

I froze in place as she shouted those words directed at me. All the women in line were now looking directly at me. She had just

Post-Reveal Adventures

humiliated me in front of at least twenty other women. But by some strange force of nature, I didn't get angry. I kept my cool, my dignity. I looked directly back at her and with a shocked look on my face and a gasp, I declared to her, "I am so sorry! My gosh. I saw the men's room on the other side of this building. I can walk you over there if you like? I know how embarrassing this must be for you."

Upon that rather brilliant comeback, about a dozen other women in line broke out in unbridled laughter. A woman standing directly behind the pretentious woman brought both of her hands up and extended both of her thumbs up and mouthed, "Oh my God! Best comeback ever."

As I continued to exit, several other women began their own positive commentary on my handling of that situation. "Way to go girl." "Good for you, and by the way, you look beautiful."

The show of support was very moving. They also stood diametrically against the verbal assault committed by this one-off miserable human being. I instinctively knew my response was the most appropriate and non-confrontational way to handle that situation. My boys, sitting just outside, heard the whole transaction. They looked at me and said, "Wow. Dad, *you are* amazing."

> I will always be their dad. That's a part of my humanity now and I embrace it completely.

Yes, they call me Dad. Just in case you're wondering, my boys will always call me Dad because I will always be *their dad*. That's a part of my humanity now and I embrace it completely. I may have been incongruent for my entire life, but I made several decisions over and over to have children.

If it weren't for my children, I wouldn't be the person I am today. Therefore, I'm more than happy that they call me Dad. And they can and will do that forever. Sure, I no longer look like a dad, nor do

Hiding From Myself

I sound like a dad, but that is who and what I was to them. I am a dad who is also a woman, and I am completely unapologetic for that.

~

By the time the movie was over, we were all exhausted just from the heat alone. We all took a vote and decided instead of eating dinner at Disney Springs, we would head back home towards Tampa and find somewhere to eat along the way.

My eldest, Corey, was set to arrive the next day. It was a wonderful feeling to know I would have all four of my boys with me after such a tough year. And to have them all around each other was even more special to me. The family dynamic that I helped to create was so splintered that it made things very difficult trying to get everyone together.

Although the boys always had a six-week summer stay, this time they would only be here for twelve days, and Corey only ten days. We didn't need to do anything extravagant. We just needed to be together. To be a family. To connect. I always found the most wonderful moments and memories come from the times when we did absolutely nothing except be together. Quality time isn't about theme parks and movies. It's about the simple things—sitting together for dinner, talking, laughing, and normal everyday boring family things.

Two nights later we went up to Moriah's house in Brooksville to see the horses and then to go to dinner at a nice Italian restaurant. Dinner was going rather well. We were seated at a nice, enormous round table with ample room for the six of us. It was actually a table in the center of the room. We were all hungry, so we ordered our drinks and dinners almost immediately. Within about ten minutes, a group of middle-aged individuals that all looked related, walked in and made their way to a table about fifteen feet from our table. There were two rather obese men who each sported beards that were doppelgangers of the guys in the band ZZ Top. The other person in the group, which I believed was a woman, sported basically the same attire as the other two. I wouldn't have even known what they looked like if they weren't staring me down. One of them was staring with glaring eyes as if he wanted to come over and hit me. It was very unnerving; troubling. So I looked right back at them with that look that says, "Not today. I don't think so."

I looked away and refocused my energy on Moriah and my kids. After about five minutes I quickly glanced over and saw that the same guy was still staring me down. It went way beyond creepy at this point. I felt danger—whether perceived or real. Enough was enough, I didn't need to feel uncomfortable. Thank God my kids had not caught on to the situation that was unfolding. I flagged down our waitress and let her know we needed our check ASAP and to bring a box for the remaining slices of enormous pizza the boys could not finish. We left without issue and that was that, and the kids did not understand what I just experienced.

The following afternoon Moriah came over and we all made our way to an exquisite outdoor mall in Wesley Chapel called Wiregrass. It's an enjoyable experience. It gives you the feel of walking down the streets of Beverly Hills.

The boys knew there was a reason we had to go to Wiregrass, and they were okay with it. Moriah and I had to make a quick pit stop into Victoria's Secret so I could get measured properly for a bra. The one I had been wearing was definitely the wrong size and very uncomfortable, and I couldn't wait any longer.

When we arrived at Victoria's Secret the boys said in near unison, "We are not going in there. We'll just stay out here."

So I replied, "We'll try to make this as fast as possible, okay?"

It's okay, we know you need to do this. We're fine, now go." Matthew said with a smile.

Upon walking in, a sales associate greeted us and got me started for my fitting. She and I left Moriah and went into the back changing rooms so she could properly fit me into the right bra. After measuring my bust size she found that the best size bra for me would be 38b. She looked at me with pleasant eyes and said, "Good for you, girl. Now, let me get you some bras that you can try on so you can tell me how they feel. Once you are ready, just call my name and I will come in and make sure it's an excellent fit."

I was so happy with the personal attention they gave me. It was definitely turning out to be an uplifting experience. After a few minutes of trying on several bras, I finally settled on three. One of them was an amazingly comfortable push-up bra she said I looked fabulous in. While the other two were your casual everyday bras, one black and one nude.

She gave me a hug upon leaving and said, "You come back anytime and I'll be happy to help you. See you soon, Amber."

Moriah had already gotten herself a few items, and she met me on the way out of the store. We noticed there had just been an incredible downpour. As we exited the store, we couldn't see the boys. I figured they went to get some cover. Then I saw them, just two stores down, completely soaked from head to toe. "Why didn't you guys just come into the store when it started raining?"

"Because it's a girl's store and we would just look like creeps."

"Oh my God, you guys are such teenagers. There were at least a dozen men in that store."

As I was shaking my head in disbelief, I looked directly across the street and saw a huge empty canvas-covered pavilion maybe one hundred feet down the street.

"Okay, so," I paused as I laughed, "then why didn't you just run across the street to the covered pavilion?"

They looked at each other and began laughing and said, "Well, I guess we didn't notice that!"

As we made our way down the street towards one of the parking lots, an older man walked towards us. From about twenty feet away until when he passed us he was glaring at me. As he passed us he said to me, "You need to get back to your mental institution. You don't belong here."

That woman that kept her composure just a few days ago at Disney Springs—yeah; remember her? Well, she had just left the building.

"No, that shit did not just happen?" I growled.

Within an instant, I told my kids and Moriah to block their ears. I turned around as he was walking away. I looked at him and I said, "Excuse me? Yeah! I'm looking at you. Why don't you say that again, asshole?" I totally lost my shit.

My head was reeling at one-thousand mile per hour. I couldn't understand it? What the fuck is wrong with people? Do they really think they need to get in your face and be hateful when they see you are different?

He kept walking as if he didn't notice me calling him out for his behavior. So at that point I just let it go, but I-was-furious.

I apologized to my kids for the language they just heard. I had to hold Matthew back from being upset with the guy. I said, "Honey, don't worry about it. Remember, I protect you, not the other way around. I shouldn't have reacted the way I just did. So I'm so sorry that you had to see that. It won't happen again."

Although I was furious, I was even more mortified that I had just lost my shit in front of my kids. I kept telling myself to just let it go. There will always be someone that's rude.

"Just let it go, you're better than that."

I would have to say that phrase over and over in my head until I got it right.

> I feel blessed to have the most amazing children in the world that love me unconditionally.

That was actually the last incident that happened. The rest of their trip was uneventful in that regard. None of that nonsense even mattered. I had my boys hugging on me. My younger son Tyler would say it's okay. I think you're pretty.

It's amazing really. I feel blessed to have the most amazing children in the world that love me unconditionally. So many transgender women lose everyone. They lose their spouses, their parents, their siblings, their relatives, and many times their own children. It's sad. And I count myself blessed that I am one of the few that has navigated this transition with the full love and support of my entire family.

~

Jack and I always had a pleasant time going to the grocery store together. Our particular grocery store name is Publix and it gives children cookies upon entering the store. He would point to the items we needed on my shopping list. At only three years old he had everything memorized from produce all the way to canned goods. He was very observant. As we approached the milk aisle and in particular where the eggs were I noticed there were quite a few people waiting to get eggs so I told Jack it would just be a minute as we waited. Out of nowhere and at the top of his little voice he asks, "Daddy? Are you a boy or a girl?"

Everyone that heard him say this had to be a little intrigued by such a question coming from a little child, so they turned around to look at me just the same as I probably would have done. So I looked him in the eyes and I said, "Well, what do you think I am, sweetheart?"

"You're my daddy, but you're also a girl. So maybe you're a boy and a girl?" He tried to explain.

"So, let's go with that, shall we?" I told him with affirming confidence. And then he kissed my arm and hugged my arm while still seated in the shopping cart and completed his thought with, "I love you so much."

So I looked right back at him and said, "No, I love you so much," and this adorable exchange repeated three or four more times as the

Post-Reveal Adventures

people that had a confused look on their face less than a minute ago were now at least slightly emotionally invested in this rather awkward but wonderful moment.

～

When my youngest son was enrolled in one of the Montessori schools, I was told by someone in my life not to go there because they wouldn't understand or take kindly to people like me. This was humiliating and dehumanizing to me. But considering I was recovering from three heart procedures, I didn't want any stress, so I agreed to pick him up at a remote location. Within a month, I had enough of the obvious prejudice that was occurring—but not at the hands of the school, rather only the person who lied to me. So I made an appointment to meet the principal and his teacher within a few days of my call. When I met the school principal, she was very welcoming and kind. She said, "Our school welcomes and understands diversity in its many forms and you are welcome here."

This touched my heart, but I was also disgusted because of the biased lies I had been told. I started introducing myself to everyone at the school. My son's teacher, other teachers, parents, and their children. Everyone was very pleasant. Did everyone "get me"? I am unsure. But no matter where they fell, they were all very nice to me.

I have spoken to many people and other parents about how sometimes dads are not men.

A wonderful example of this in action was during a school event called "Daddy's Day." As I entered the building, I saw some dads already in line standing with their young children. They were waiting to go into their child's respective classrooms. As our even visitation had it, his mom brought him to the school that morning. He was standing at the end of the hallway next to his classroom door at the front of this forming line. As he saw me make the turn to his hallway, he excitedly yelled at the top of his lungs, "Daddy! Daddy!" as he ran toward me with his arms wide open.

This cute display got the attention of all the other dads as they watched this little boy run up to a woman that he called Dad. It seemed to confuse some of them, while others knew I was transgender. But not one of them was anything but courteous. I'm not afraid and I'm not self-conscious. Not anymore.

I leaned down and gave him an enormous hug. Then I stood up and noticed that two of his friends had left the arms of their dads to come over to my son and began hugging my leg just like he was. I found it ironic and a little unexpected because I didn't know these children very well. But the experience was beyond cute.

So what was my takeaway from these experiences with my youngest son's school? An understanding that there are just some people in this world that will always be toxic with certain things they don't want to understand. And that's okay. But it also showed me that there are countless more individuals and families that understand and know how to treat another human being, no matter what their circumstance in life.

> I'm not afraid and I'm not self-conscious. Not anymore.

So am I angry? No. Why should I be? I survived and recovered from an ischemic stroke. I weathered three heart procedures that fixed a congenital heart defect and put me back on track to living my best life.

And that best life would not be possible if not for the professionals and caring teams at Baycare Medical Group Cardiology, and in particular, Dr. James Irwin, MD. and Dr. Sai, MD of the Renal Hypertension Center, both in Tampa, FL. Everyone that cared for me, whether in the office or one of my many stays at St. Joseph's Hospital; from nursing to reception and from surgical staff to billing, you all had genuine caring, compassion, and empathy to say, "This woman will recover so she can complete her transition, especially if we have anything to say about it." So to all of you I met and befriended at both practices and the hospital, I love every one of you for your support and friendly conversations. But most of all, for being who you are!

There is one other person that affected me profoundly while in St. Joseph's Hospital. He is the Hospital's Pastor. He understood I was transgender and had become religiously agnostic. Despite my trepidation of what may occur during his visit, I welcomed him into my room. He was the most caring, empathetic pastor I had ever met in all of my days. In fact, when I told him of my emergency room conflict concerning misgendering, he went back to his office and printed a huge banner, brought it back to my room, where he hung it just above the bed's headboard. It read, "Please call me, Amber."

We sat for an hour and got to know each other and ended up holding hands and praying together. It was an uplifting experience for me, and possibly God's way of saying, "Not all people within the man-made construct of religion are ignorant." Thank you, Pastor, for giving me renewed hope and faith in at least part of the religious community.

Not everyone is nice, however. When you're transgender, every day is a day where you must keep your guard up. My short stories of adversity pale in comparison to the enormity of adversity other segments within my demographic face. For some tragic reason, trans women of color seem to be targeted disproportionately to the rest of us. So keep in mind that when reading my experiences, that there are trans women living in perpetual fear and far more guarded than even I. I truly wish certain people within our society could be less confrontational and aggressive towards people like us that sets off their "little boy" insecurities. These men attacking us are not men. They are insecure cowards.

Every few days, I would go to my local Wawa to get a fresh salad or a half turkey sandwich without bread. I usually avoid this particular Wawa late at night, but I was starving. While waiting to retrieve my order, one of the few people in the store; a rather shaggy, unkept man approached me. He walked right up beside me and stared with a dangerous look in his eyes.

"What da fuck you 'spossed to be? You hea' me? What da *fuck* you 'spossed to be!"

He was now inches from my face, and the few people in the store now had eyes on the situation.

"Get away from me, and leave me alone." I demanded.

I was scared to death. But he did back away, shaking his head saying, "Wow. You a freak! You a God damn freak!"

He then exited the store and stood outside the window staring at me. I became more and more anxious with each passing second. Then the clerk, who witnessed the whole thing, told me a sheriff was walking in and I might want to get his attention.

I quickly began walking toward the sheriff as the man pulled away from the window and before I even reached the officer, had already ran down the block and nearly out of sight. The officer looked at me, noticing panic in my eyes, and asked, "Is everything ok?"

I don't know why, but I decided to just let well enough alone and replied, "Yeah. Um. Yes. I'm sorry."

As I walked away from the officer, something in me knew I had made the right decision. I had heard far too many personal stories about the police discriminating against us transgender women. Jeering, constant misgendering, manhandling, and just about every other form of transphobia they could display. Worse, they would always place transgender women in the male population, which far too many times resulted in assault and rape within the walls of the jail.

Post-Reveal Adventures

So yeah, thanks; but no thanks. I got this.

Each day, we face the world with the courage and fortitude that many people will never possess. Why? Because we deserve to exist. We didn't get a say in this. We didn't "sign-up" or get a full-ride scholarship to Transgender University. Each one of us has to find that place within each of us. That place that allows you to shout, "I am me! Just as you are you. Am I different? Yes. Are you? You bet your ass. All of us are in one way or another. Our difference just happens to be in an area that for some reason makes some of you as uncomfortable AF.

We are blessed to now live in a time where former President Barack Obama brought to the forefront a national conversation about transgender issues. We live in a time where the entire medical community, mass media, fortune 500 companies, families, friends, and strangers are embracing the fact that we have been misunderstood because of stale, untruthful mythology. We live in a time when movies and TV series like *The Danish Girl, Pose, Transparent, I am Jazz, Orange is the New Black, Disclosure*, and many others have numerous Emmy Awards and massive viewership.

People are learning about things that were once inaccessible and hidden.

Now that we've gotten that out of the way, let's take a look at how the universe revealed it was time to inject a healthy dose of irony into my life, and right when I needed it. If only I could have been a fly on the wall . . .

Karma
A Dish Best Served with a Healthy Side of Irony

Oh, how I have waited for a glimmer of poetic justice for what Aaron did to me so many years ago in high school. I've been told, "Sometimes life is stranger than fiction." And you know what? I don't think I could have ever thought this one up in a thousand years. It was certainly poetic.

It was September 20, 2019, and I was just finishing up a conversation with one of my girlfriends when I received a Facebook Messenger *wave* from an old friend from my hometown; someone I've not spoken to in nearly a decade. We were friends since the first years of Facebook, but we rarely, if ever, communicated. In fact, it had been so long since we had talked that neither of us would have even remembered we were Facebook friends.

I told her there was a guy from my hometown trying to reconnect with me. Her only response was, "Go get 'em tigress."

"Oh no, no, no, not him. It's definitely not like that. But remember when I told you about Aaron? Well, this guy is best friends with Aaron. So at least the conversation could be interesting," as I giggled.

"Hi, Brandon. I noticed you waved at me."

"Hi. Yeah, I did. How are you?"

"I'm good. It's nice to hear from you after so many years." I replied.

"Where are you living?" he asked.

"I've been in Tampa for nearly ten years now."

Then he responded with, "Yes," of all things.

"Yes, what? Yes, you agree I live in Tampa? LOL."

He paused for several minutes, so I figured the conversation was over.

"What are you doing now? Do you want to talk?"

"I'm just sitting here. Sure, I'd love to talk. Is there something you want to talk about?"

"Great! Maybe . . . " he replied after a brief pause. For someone that wanted to talk, he was certainly not off to a brilliant start. After another painfully long pause, he came back with, "I'd like to have a private conversation if that's okay. You know what I mean, right?"

Something inside of me instinctively knew this conversation was about to go south—fast. "Oh, shit!" I thought. "Did he just ask me what I think he just asked me? Oh God, I don't think Brandon knows who I am."

> I knew that he probably saw my new profile picture, my new legal name, and liked what he saw.

My mind was running in overdrive because I knew that he probably saw my new profile picture, my new legal name, and liked what he saw.

"So, can we talk privately? It'll be fun. I love your profile pic, by the way!"

"Yep. He's going there. Oh, my God, If I say yes this will not end well." I thought. "He's totally hitting on me in the strangest way and wants to have a *private* chat."

While it seemed like it would be fun to fuck with him just a little, I instead asked him if he truly remembers me. But before I did that,

Karma: A Dish Best Served with a Healthy Side of Irony

I had to be sure that was where he was going with this conversation. So I boldly asked, "I'd love to have a private conversation. How do you want this to work?"

A few minutes later he responded just as I thought he would, "We can work this out any way you want to. Your profile picture is hot."

I thanked him for the compliment, but I also just confirmed my instincts were correct, so I asked him one more question.

"Brandon, you don't remember me do you?" I asked.

"Actually no. But I am trying to remember. Who were the friends you hung out with? I'm really sorry. I should definitely remember someone especially like you."

"Okay, so we had many mutual friends. For example, your best friend, Aaron. I also know your sister."

"Really? You know Aaron and my sister? Wow. I should definitely know you."

"Hun, do you remember anyone in Liberty with the last name of Washington?"

"Sure. This guy Eddie. But he left a while ago," he recalled.

"Brandon, my name used to be Eddie. I thought you knew I was a transgender woman. Everyone up there knows. It mystifies me you don't in such a tiny town."

"Wait. What! You're Eddie? Bullshit. And no, I didn't know."

"No. It's me. I transitioned here in Florida."

It was then that everything went silent. He disappeared. Within minutes, I noticed he had unfriended me. He was a married man who just got tagged trying to have a private chat with some woman he found attractive, and now he had to run away as quickly as possible.

I called my girlfriend back and told her what had just transpired. She laughed, "Oh girl, he was definitely trying to have a little *fun*. Yeah, I've had my share of them."

I wanted so badly to be a fly on the wall the next day just to hear Brandon tell Aaron about what happened. I knew he'd tell Aaron because they had been best friends for so many years and both, at least before they were married, had been fulfilling their conquests with various women since graduation. I could just hear him when he and Aaron were alone.

"Aaron, you are not going to fucking believe what happened last night, man. I was starting a chat with this chick and it turns out the chick was Eddie Washington; Amber Washington."

Oh, to see Aaron's face turn into a pale shade of gray while choking on his own saliva upon hearing that his best friend just made a pass at one of his first conquests so many years ago. Aaron's response would have probably been something like, *Gulp*, "Um wow. Are you sure? Oh. Well, um, did he, I mean, she say anything else to you? Anything about anyone else, perhaps?"

"Wait, you knew? Why didn't you ever tell me?" Brandon would respond.

Oh, the sweet irony. The discomfort of a scandalous and long-forgotten relationship had just resurfaced and Aaron, knowing he could never let on that he and I had a thing back in high school, must have looked as uncomfortable as a pig on ice.

I always knew karma is a dish best served with a healthy side of irony.

Stalled in Transition: Part II

By the end of January, I had everything scheduled and locked in. That's when I began hearing about a virus named *COVID-19 coronavirus,* which originated in China. The chatter was growing quickly as they learned how fast this virus was spreading inside Wuhan, in the Hubei province of China. The world was quickly coming to terms with the idea that this could become a global pandemic in weeks. On January 21st, the United States reported its first case. By January 30th, The World Health Organization (WHO) declared a global health emergency. And just a month later, on February 29, the United States had its first death related to COVID-19.

Within a few weeks, nearly the entire planet began practicing social distancing and isolation. It was beyond frightening; it was surreal. To see the streets of major cities all around the world deserted was like watching something out of any post-apocalyptic movie. To see downtown Manhattan, the bustling financial center of America turned into a ghost town, instantly brought *nearly* everyone into the mindset that our world had just transformed. We were living in a true-to-life Stephen King novel.

Also within the month of March, all that I had set back into motion and rescheduled to reboot my transition had all disappeared within less than a week. All non-essential and elective surgeries were postponed indefinitely. I also began hearing that it may not even be until the end of 2021 before life even remotely goes back to what it was before this new year. Yep, 2020 had begun—shitty.

As the news of a nationwide shutdown, state by state, was being received, people were busy doing what they typically do—panicking. Even the best scientific minds cannot figure out why everyone furiously raced to hoard toilet paper? Out of all the essential supplies one needs, they all chose toilet paper? I suppose the news of this pandemic scared the shit out of a lot of people, literally. But the hoarding did not stop there. Soon there were shortages of nearly everything and grocery stores needed to impose maximums of two on certain types of items.

All the hoarding and irrational behavior aside, the actual issues with COVID-19 are that it has proven difficult to manage the incubation period, which ranges from four to fourteen days. There is no vaccine as yet for this new strain of the coronavirus, although research institutions and companies around the world are working feverishly (forgive the pun) to develop a vaccine, along with therapeutics that can help save the infected. The people that have the highest risk of life-threatening complications because of COVID-19 are the elderly, especially those over seventy and people that are immunocompromised or have several other serious health concerns.

Because of my recent health issues this past year, I am considered high risk. Therefore, I have self-isolated and completely avoid any contact with other individuals.

COVID-19 will complicate life for me until they develop a vaccine and mass immunizations begin. The latest data suggest the earliest viable candidate for a vaccine may not be until the first months of 2021. This means that when autumn begins and flu season ramps up, we may be in for a much larger issue than the first wave.

Stalled in Transition: Part II

By the time you read this, so much more will have happened, so I will just leave this topic with the following narrative.

Here I am, for the second time, stalled in my transition. It was bad enough going through what I went through last year wondering if I'd even be around for the next year. But now I have to worry about contracting a virus that is potentially deadly for someone like me. My immune system is still not up to par. On top of this, I have recent conflicting test results that suggest I may have lupus.

Now all I can do is sit inside my house, and isolate from the rest of the world as best I can. I stopped grocery shopping in person. Instead, I began using an online app. I have groceries not out-of-stock delivered directly and left at my front door.

My saving grace is I have equal joint legal and physical custody of my youngest son. So every other week for seven straight days we can be creative together. We can be a family. I call my other boys each day just to tell them I love them and to hear their voices if nothing else.

As I write this book, I am still in isolation. There are still many empty shelves at every grocery store. People don't know how to self-isolate, let alone do it for lengthy periods of time. It is that reaction that will make this virus spread deeper and deeper into our communities and make the isolation process exponentially longer. Many states have also begun to lift certain social isolation restrictions as many businesses reopen.

I am living in a time that will go down in history books much like the Spanish flu of 1918. It's frightening not knowing what your future might or might not hold.

Although frightened, I focus on and attempt to put out positivity into the world around me. Each day I continue to take baby steps forward along my complicated journey. I have begun to face each new challenge with a freshness and determination that once eluded me.

> *"Never frown when facing new challenges. Instead, focus on the ones you've overcome, and smile down on the ones you've yet to conquer."*

No matter the severity, we should all face new challenges in life from this perspective. When we recall the challenges we have overcome, it makes it far easier to face the new ones laid before us.

Takeaway

I no longer hesitate for one second to admit that I have made several mistakes in my life and inadvertently hurt some people along the way; just as they hurt me. But when one looks at causality, the brunt of the burden rests upon me, not them. The fact is, I wanted to fit in so badly that I faked most of my natural life to live what I thought was a "normal" life—whatever the hell that means?

I couldn't bear to live a life filled with relentless mocking, or the possibility of something more dangerous. I didn't want to be one of those people you'd see on daytime talk shows. I wasn't some *sideshow freak* born for everyone's entertainment. I wasn't someone seeking attention. I was just a normal everyday girl with the wrong goddamned anatomy and not a single tool in my toolbox that could help me navigate this ridiculous conundrum.

Approximately 99.3% of the population are born congruent. And you could read this book, and several others like it, and still not completely understand what it is to be transgender. To have a brain physically formed one way and a body that has formed diametrically opposed to that brain is mind-boggling for many people—even myself. But it happens. It leaves you feeling less human; less capable of being able to experience life like everyone else. Many of us transition, in a variety of ways, but that only gets us a little closer to being congruent. The truth is no matter how much we transition we will never be completely congruent; at least not the way we should have been the day we were born. But transitioning has been an absolute lifesaver within the transgender community, without question.

> "**Hiding from** yourself is nothing more than a vain attempt to satisfy the perception others have of you, rather than embracing **the wonder of you.**"

Speaking about the wonder of you; let me tell you of a very recent incident that involved one of my best friends, Rebecca. An incident that just about all of us transgender women experience that may leave you with a little bit more empathy.

Rebecca and I can talk for hours every day and we do. It's almost a problem. But seriously, one day she called to let me know how confident and great she felt about herself as she was making her way out for the day. She's one of those women that possesses qualities many of us envy. We have a word we often use to describe a trans woman that physically passes as cisgender—"stealth."

I was so happy she felt beautiful and confident, because although physically "stealth" she has always been self-conscious about the damage testosterone had done to her pharynx. She was hyper-aware that her voice often had people profile her wrongly, no matter how completely feminine her features were.

Rebecca had not yet embarked on the next part of her journey; voice therapy. She has the mindset that her voice will never sound feminine; the same exact horrible thought I had less than a year before writing this book. Remember, I had a voice deeper than James Earl

Jones. I was a concert voice-over artist for crying out loud! You don't get more masculine vocally than that.

We all have different things we wish to adjust to rid ourselves of the testosterone damage. Hers was currently hyper-focused on her voice. Just a few hours later, she called in complete despondency. Between her tears, she told me that she was at the store checking out a few moments earlier when the cashier blurted, "So did you find everything, Sir?"

Instead of correcting him, she decided to simply nod. Many of us become passive in these types of situations, and rather than disputing being misgendered, we internalize the event. That's why I love her so much, because she doesn't want to hurt anybody or get into confrontations with anyone. She always assumes the best in people.

"He must have made a mistake. Anyway, I'm really not worthy of Miss or Ma'am anyway," she said.

That's another thing that happens to us. We become so disconnected through our own self-deprecation that our own existence becomes meaningless. Much of the self-deprecation stems from words, and in this case the word was, "Sir." That one word set into motion a series of events that led to her desperately calling me for comfort.

When I finally got back to her, a half hour had already passed from the incident. I wasn't there for her when she needed me most. I felt guilty and horrible because I know all too well the pain that ensues after such an encounter.

She had been sitting in her car weeping and wanting to give up. She asked herself, "What's the point? Is all of this really worth it? People are never going to change. Stealth? I'm not fucking stealth!"

The experience had once again taken its toll on her emotionally. That's the thing most cisgender folks don't understand about us. When we are misgendered or deadnamed (calling us by our old given name), it can change your whole day. It rips into your humanity and damages your sense of self. Whether it occurs as an honest mistake or is done egregiously, misgendering and deadnaming both have serious emotional consequences that affect our mental well-being.

Rebecca's experience is common within our community. It is one I have experienced countless times. It's never fun, never easy to navigate, and never ends well internally.

Although she said her experience was brought on by her voice, we all need to be cognizant of the reality that the human condition is so much more diverse than many ever knew. But along with that, we, as transgender women, need to have tools in order to cope with the enormous pain associated with misgendering and deadnaming. We have to love ourselves completely—regardless. After giving her a huge virtual hug, I shared these words with her. Words from an inspirational quote I wrote several years earlier.

> *"Do you want everlasting love?*
> *Fall in love with the person who adores you from within.*
> ***She is you.****"*

So what about all of you that are not transgender, what can you take away from my story?

Self-Awareness: Each one of us is on a journey to discover and become our best self; our best version. We require this to experience and live a truly fulfilled life. For many of us, part of this discovery will be to experience the unconditional love of a child or another human being.

For nearly all of us, it is the recognition of our individual flaws. To understand our ego—and no, the ego is not the bad rap we give it. The ego is not synonymous with being entitled or arrogant. Rather, the ego is the mediator between our conscious and unconscious self. Your ego can be your best friend or your worst enemy. For me, my ego became my enemy, my ill-conceived illusion of self. I allowed my rational and irrational fears, along with many insecurities, to steal my freedom. It was my ego that led me to so many repeated mistakes in my life. However, it was also my ego that led me to one of the greatest achievements in my life—living authentically. The evolutionary and successful development of self-awareness is key to developing empathy, or to understand the emotions of another.

Empathy: Hopefully, you have gained a greater sense of empathy, or perhaps it has become a newly discovered sense within you. To understand, on a deeper level, the emotional side of something you've never had to think about is huge. It shows to both yourself and the world around you, that you see that life and struggle exist outside of the bubble each one of us lives within. So, begin to listen, but not with your ears.

Wisdom: Perhaps you have learned something that once was a mystery to you, or even first taught to you to be an illusion, fake, or a sin. You understand the human condition is not as simple as some would have you believe. That the human condition is extremely diverse on a multitude of levels. And what we learned in eighth-grade biology is not the end of the story, but merely the introduction to it. It's sort of like taking basic math, then telling the world you understand The Calculus. Math is math, right?

You have learned that many individuals that are transgender transition late in life for a variety of reasons, including the stigma of dealing with an ancient, rigid societal construct of sex and gender, or their children they had from conforming.

Make no mistake, society is one of the hardest obstacles to overcome when needing to transition or be authentic. The lack of acceptance of never receiving affirmation from family, friends, or others; or worse, the dehumanizing treatment received by those very individuals is the leading cause of the insanely high suicide rates within my community. Many would have you believe it's because "trans people are mental."

Ideologies and misinformation lead to these things, and many of us find it too convenient for the bubble we live within to ignore them. While I chose to be free of religious ideologies, that doesn't mean you should. Each one of us is on our own journey and each one of us will have a unique way of experiencing our own true authenticity and genuine happiness and closeness to our creator or whatever your belief may or may not be.

> *"If we view ideology as an opinion rather than an assumed fact, the world becomes more beautiful and its people more relatable."*

For those of you that are transgender, out of the closet or what I call the deep, dark, dank basement, my advice to you is to understand your surroundings. We still live in a world where there is great divisiveness in our societies. Divisiveness built upon age-old religious mythology and run-amok political misinformation campaigns. Why? Simple. Trans people are inconvenient. We make up a tiny percentage of the overall population that might cost the "taxpayers" (which you may be one of) additional money. And then there are those that stand against diversity. And those that pick which components of medical science they deem to be forever "static." Newsflash, everything within medical science is forever changing and *never* static.

Do yourself a favor and be as authentic as you can. And do it when you are ready. Looking back, however, I'd say to myself, "Don't put it off another single day. We have only this life to live. And later in your life, you will flood yourself with regret and loss for what you didn't allow yourself to live."

For those of you that are parents of a child that is transgender. Whether you are empathetic and understanding of their needs, make sure you are fully integrated into a professional therapeutic process for all of you. Because this is not about you—it's about your child. For too long society has made us believe that somehow, magically, the parent knows best who a child is or how they identify. Experience has shown us with immeasurable confidence that the only person on the planet that knows who that child is, *is the child themselves*.

~

To anyone else that has taken the time to read this, I deeply and sincerely thank you. For you to have read this far shows me you have an open mind to understanding something that many people until recently didn't even know existed. Then there are others that still assume it's some demonic possession, sin, or breach of some fictitious contract with God.

We have come such a long way in the past few years, yet; we have allowed many within our society to inject bias, hatred, and mythology back into the equation. When we hear about these injustices, we must stop telling each other that, "They'll never change. So don't bother trying to educate them." While it may be statistically correct, it is not always the case. Maybe I am more unique than I give myself credit for because I've been able to emotionally and intellectually reach many people that many within my community have called "a waste of time."

Hiding From Myself

Many years ago, being transgender coincided with having a mental health issue. Like everything in this life, medical science's recent discoveries finally eradicated that outdated idea across the globe. Yet, many people still hold on to old truths that were never true. Being transgender is a mixture of things within the disciplines of neurology, genetics, and endocrinology, among others. We also have discovered that there seems to be something that happens during gestation—in my case, during the second half of my mom's pregnancy. It's not something any of us ever want to be, it's just something we always were.

~

I hope that you have learned something from a person that has made so many wrong choices in their life because of who they are. I was a person mortally afraid to expose my authentic self to the world. But as this religiously agnostic, but spiritual woman will tell you, God put her right where she needed to be. The people introduced into her life happened right when and where she needed them. I can say the same about myself affecting others' lives too.

Since revealing my true self to the world, I have had countless individuals speak to me about how my life has become inspirational for so many people, and a learning experience for others. While I thank everyone for their compliments, I am just one of the countless voices in a sea of incongruity. There are individuals that suffer tremendous suffering every day, and most of that suffering is caused by other people and society.

I am also so proud of some of you that came forward and told me that because of my story you have decided to come out of the closet. Bravo! Congratulations for ending a vicious cycle of trying to conform to some other person's idea of what you are supposed to be. Continue to face your life with unapologetic determination each and every day.

As for me? I am still a work in progress. I am still working diligently to drink my own Kool-Aid. I have been called the queen of self-deprecation. That is a challenge I have yet to overcome, but no doubt will. As a woman that desires genuine love in her life, I know I must remove myself from my own negative influence and manifest pure positive energy. The more I manifest, the more that becomes a genuine possibility. So I made a promise to myself.

> *"I promise to breathe in fresh hope each day, knowing **hope is the promise of life.**"*
> *"Breathe in that good ass prana baby!"*

Wait? You don't know about prana? Okay, quickly. Prana, in Hindu philosophy, is the life-giving universal force or energy that flows in and around the body. We often refer to taking in prana when we breathe deeply or eat healthy foods; thus absorbing the positive energies of the earth and heavens. So, "breathe in that good ass prana baby" is your permanent homework assignment.

That prana has given me new hope. And that *new hope* has coincidentally brought me to Dr. Christine McGinn's Papillon Center in **New Hope**, Pennsylvania. This is where I will take a major step along my journey to becoming congruent. After two postponements due to my health and the COVID-19 pandemic, I have been scheduled for my long awaited gender confirmation surgery (vaginoplasty and labiaplasty) only two days after my birthday on August 4, 2020. "Happy *new* birthday to me."

Hiding From Myself

For some, adversity seems to stay one step ahead of you no matter how many times you've already overcome it. This couldn't present itself to be truer than with the news I received exactly two weeks to the moment from my upcoming surgery.

After visiting my doctor to further investigate why I have been losing so much hair so suddenly, they found what they believe to be cancer on my right breast. After facing so much adversity in my life, especially health-related adversity, I was once again faced with a new and frightening challenge and major decision.

I've been running this marathon with undying determination and courage for so long. I can see the finish line right in front of me. I can taste victory, if only I could cross that finish line. But today, my legs seemed to have given out from beneath me. The information, as limited as it was, sent me into a violent, uncoordinated emotional free fall. "The finish line is right there. It's right there in front of me!" I cried.

All of the personal triumphs I've experienced, especially in the past few years have been replaced with yet another round of heavy contemplation of my own mortality. My new challenge; my new fear is not of what I must now endure and overcome, but rather, of how my four children, and in particular, my youngest, Jack would feel if I was no longer here.

No longer can I afford to be *hiding from myself*, from adversity, or from an uncertain future. I have finally blossomed into who I was always meant to be, so now is not the time to give up. And it is definitely not the time to waste another day waiting for "me" to arrive. Because, she's always been here, and she is much stronger than she thinks!

My children are the truest extension of me. They are my lifeblood. No matter the future, I know this. I want them to know that they are and eternally will be, loved beyond anything I can put into English diction. So these final thoughts are dedicated to my most precious loves, Corey, Matthew, Tyler, and Jack.

I may have turned out to be a different kind of dad; a dad that the world will in the near future completely embrace as just another part of the diverse human condition—a dad that also happens to be a woman. To some, that may still feel a bit weird or awkward, but not to my boys. No. They understand unconditional love and that each of us are born unique. But they also know and have learned that adversity leads to empathy, and empathy leads to unconditional love.

My determination and strength through years of adversity that took a lifetime to overcome has shown me things I would have never seen if I hadn't been born incongruent.

Remember, no matter the adversity you face in life—self-love and determination are the keys to successfully overcoming it. Self-love and determination will carry you through the most difficult of challenges. So if you take away one thing from this book, let it be this quote about determination.

> *"If you are no longer able to run across that finish line, fall to the ground and roll through it instead."*

For now, my journey continues just as yours will for you. Our respective journeys continue into our next existence; whatever that is. I believe we are on a multidimensional journey; one we never complete. We live inside of a multidimensional continuum as immortal beings temporarily trapped within a three-dimensional experience.

As such, my wish is for each of you is to grow in self-awareness, empathy, wisdom, spirituality, and most importantly; to love yourself for the wonder that you are.

Last, but not least; no matter what race, culture, religion, sexual orientation, or gender identity you represent, remember we are all on the same journey, just on different roads. But know this, my

Hiding From Myself

friends, they all lead to the same destination. So love yourself. Love one another. And remember to seize every opportunity you can to do something good for somebody.

Acknowledgments

There would be no book to write if it were not for my parents. During my younger years, it was my mom who tried her very best to understand the complex struggle I faced each day. And since coming out, my dad has been my rock. Dad, you have stood by my side and have been watching me blossom into the woman I was always meant to be. You have done so with unconditional love and support, and that is overwhelming and beautiful. The day you first called me your "daughter" was one that will live in its own special place in my heart forever. Thank you for listening to the countless drafts of this book during its evolution. I love you so much!

I owe a debt of gratitude to a longtime friend, colleague, and literary expert Sari Rosenheck. Without her initial guidance, I might still be the "run-on sentence queen of the world." Thank you Sari!

I would also like to thank Moriah Ritterman for her remarkable friendship and support as she listened to my seemingly endless rewrites every week. I would also like to thank Cesar Broncas for your lessons on conversational Spanish needed within this work. Gracias mi amigo!

I would especially like to thank the women within the transgender communities of Tampa and St. Petersburg, Florida. You ladies are truly remarkable. Kimberly Kuntz and Paula Hull, the two of you have been there for me during my entire transition. You are both true shining lights in my life and I am blessed to have friends like you. I would also like to thank Anthony Cascio, because without his dedicated friendship and quick action during my stroke, I may not have been here to write this book in the first place.

Finally, I would like to thank all of the trans women that came before me, that paved the way to a brighter future for all transgender people. Pioneers like Sylvia Rivera, Miss Major Griffin-Gracy, Victoria Cruz, and Marsha Johnson. I can exist because of your determination to step out from the shadows and begin a movement. Without these ladies I wouldn't even be here to write this book.

About the Author

Amber Rose Washington is an author, songwriter, musician, producer, public speaker, and advocate for trans girls and women. Although her greatest passion has always been music, writing books has become a very suitable segue into the next chapter of her life.

Amber grew up in Liberty, New York; a small town in the Catskill Mountains. Her town and region were the inspiration behind the movie, *Dirty Dancing*. "The Catskills" are well-known by the Hollywood elite as the place where so many celebrities of the past got their big break. You can experience a glimpse into this region in the Netflix Original series, *The Marvelous Mrs. Maisel*.

Her early accomplishments include working in the mid-90s as an arranger and cowriter on an exhibit that brought attention to the children of Africa; most notably, in Ethiopia. After traveling to over 150 countries, this exhibit would find its home in the Smithsonian in Washington, DC.

She had her true introduction into the music business from the late Ann Ruckert, who was the Vice President of the Board of Governors of the Grammy's and vocal coach to the top names in the industry. While she wrote many genres of music, it was her smooth jazz that people would come to recognize.

Before coming out, Amber also worked with several members of HBO's, *The Sopranos* and the movie *Goodfellas* in the capacity of producer. She has also worked with numerous country music recording artists doing TV and radio voice-overs, stage management, and live concert introductions.

Amber has always surrounded herself with incredibly successful and influential people, from songwriters and musicians to Hollywood actors and screenwriters.

She attributes her final amassment of courage required to live her life authentically to former President Barack Obama and his positive words and actions toward the transgender community.

Amber currently lives in Florida. She and her team are currently building out her platform which will allow her to bring greater awareness to the diversity of the human condition. This platform will also facilitate innovative and educational speaking engagements and interactive lectures at college universities, pride events, radio, Internet-based, and TV interviews, as well as regional transgender support group outreach in the United States and beyond.

For more information on interviewing or booking Amber for an interview or speaking engagement, please visit: ***amberrosewashington.com.***

www.ingramcontent.com/pod-product-compliance
Lightning Source LLC
Chambersburg PA
CBHW021144080526
44588CB00008B/206